Thank you
supporting my dream!

THE WIDOW

NEXT DOOR

Learning to live again as a young widow
and single mom after
losing my husband to suicide

Heather Cruz

HEATHER CRUZ

ISBN-13: 978-1981743469

ISBN-10: 1981743464

Edited by Lisa Condora www.condoracontent.com

Publishing services provided by:

I dedicate this book in loving memory to my husband,
Alexander Cruz.

July 6, 1983 - December 31, 2012

FOREWORD

Heather and I met in seventh grade. We quickly became good friends and had the opportunity to reach many milestones as time went by. We basically grew up and experienced so much together. We attended graduations, lots of birthday celebrations, basement parties, pool parties, proms, bridal showers, weddings, baby showers, 5Ks, and much more. One of my favorite traditions is our annual trip to the county fair every July. We have countless memories that I hold very close to my heart.

Heather, Alex, my husband at the time, and I used to go on double dates often. Our favorite date night was going out to dinner for hibachi. That was our thing, the four of us. Dinner was often followed by a silly Walmart trip or something random. I remember one night when the boys turned an empty parking lot into a playground of their own, playing baseball with an inflatable bat that was randomly found in one of our cars.

Let me preface by saying that I would never ever compare these two situations. Heather and I both had no idea at the time, but we found out on the same exact night that we would both be starting new lives in 2013. The big difference is that my new life was my choice.

On that same New Year's Eve of 2012, I came home early from work unexpectedly and found out that my husband at the time was cheating. I could have ignored it and moved on with our life together, but he had refused to cut off contact with the other woman, so we ultimately decided to get divorced. When I got the news about Alex, I tried to contact him right away since Alex was such an important person to the both of us. After hours of unsuccessfully trying to reach him, I was forced to deliver the news to him in a text message.

We traveled to Delaware separately to attend the funeral. I remember that I begged my soon-to-be ex-husband to wear his wedding ring that day in front of our friends because I didn't want anyone to figure out what was going on in our lives yet. We were there to pay respects to Alex. I wanted to focus on Heather and Alexa, and chose to forget about my own problems for just that one day.

Heather and I spoke almost every single day after that traumatic night. As time went on, we realized that a lot of the feelings we both were experiencing were similar, even though our situations were totally different. Throughout it all, Heather proved herself time and time again to be an amazing friend and was always there for me, which was especially selfless with everything she was going through. She was one of the most supportive people during my divorce, and I was supportive for her as well.

To bring you up to date, I got through my divorce with no major issues. We had to sell our house, so I moved closer to where I work. I spent some time in weekly therapy sessions, which really helped me. Luckily, I also got full custody of our pets and I felt safer living by myself in a new town with my German Shepherd, Kona, by my side. I got married to a wonderful man in July of 2016. Although I went through some major hurdles, I think I'm exactly where I'm supposed to be right now and I'm happy.

I am not going to say much more to bring you up to date with Heather's life; you'll just have to read this book and learn more about her journey. No spoiler alerts! I can tell you this much though. Over the past five years, I have seen Heather, a person I met when we were just adolescent pre-teens, overcome something unimaginable. She is one of the strongest people I know, and her strength has not only helped her get through this, it has helped me as well. I'm sure it will help many of you out there reading this right now.

Let me end with this quote, which is one of my favorites. "You never know how strong you are until being strong is the only choice you have." We all go through a lot of hardships in our lives, whether we're open about it or silent. I truly believe that you are never given more than you can handle and everything life throws your way only makes you stronger. Have you ever found yourself in a situation where you even surprised yourself at how well you handled it? I know that happens to me, not all the time, but it definitely does once in a while. No matter what you are going through in your life at this moment, we should always remember that this is just one moment in your life and things will get better. They always do.

Being a part of this book has meant the world to me and I thank Heather for this opportunity. I wholeheartedly support her cause and the heartfelt message of this book. Throughout the past five years, I have seen firsthand at what an amazing mom Heather is, how hard-working and driven she is, and how she has grown as a person. I hope you enjoy reading about Heather's journey and learn from her example of strength and perseverance.

~ **Lisa Condora**

It was New Year's Eve 2012 and little did I know, that evening, my life was about to change forever. I was married to the man I believed to be my soul mate and best friend. After years of heartbreak with miscarriages and infertility struggles, we were finally blessed with our little girl, just seven months earlier. That life-changing moment ultimately led me to a life of widowhood and single motherhood. This is the journal of my life after losing the love of my life to mental illness and suicide. Early in the journey, writing became an avenue to express my thoughts and feelings. Now, it has become a way to help others travelling a similar path as I am, open the doors to a conversation about the reality of suicide, its impact, and bring light to the stigma associated with it. My name is Heather and this is my story.

I have always considered myself the "average" but "not-so-average" girl. I grew up in New Jersey, in a great town, not far, but far enough from the Jersey Shore. We lived close enough to take day trips to the shore and had the opportunity to spend our prom weekend in Wildwood. Still, we weren't close enough to walk to the boardwalk just to play some arcade games. Many days and nights were spent at the local mall, movie theaters, and of course some of the the best diners in the world! I'd say I was the rather typical kid growing up in New Jersey in the late '90s and early 2000s. Just living in America at the end of the millennium.

I was never one of the popular kids, but I guess you could say I was in the meaty part of the curve. I did have a lot of friends growing up. I should say, I still HAVE a lot of friends. About fifteen years after high school, I still have some of the most amazing friends a woman could ask for. Even though I don't live in New Jersey anymore, my high school friends have stayed with me through the best and worst moments of my life, and everything in between. Throughout college and my adult life, I have only added to that amazing group of friends.

I was never a big dater and spent a lot of time in the "friend zone" with many guys. It was not until the end of high school that things started to pick up. I still was not very good at it. I'm not sure I would say I was GOOD at it at any point in my life. Though anyone close to me would describe me as the absolute outgoing social butterfly, it has its limits. Or maybe just one limit: insecurity.

My parents moved to Delaware within weeks after I graduated high school. I can't help but think of the (now annoying) catch-phrase "Dela Where?" With so many changes occurring at once, I felt like my life was over! I would soon be leaving for college and come "home" to NOTHING on school breaks. I would have no friends and no place to hang out. Nothing (or at least that was my perception of it all). I was devastated to say the least, having to say goodbye to the house where I had spent the first eighteen years of my life. In order to spend the last few weeks of my summer in New Jersey before moving away to college, I moved my stuff to a friend's house on the other side of "my" town.

What an amazing summer it was! I was dating and partying, going to the beach, and staying up all night playing cards and drinking coffee at the local twenty-four hour diner. I spent those few weeks thoroughly enjoying the summer and working at the mall. It was the best time with the best of friends! At last, the dreadful day came. It was the day I had to move to Delaware. My friends came to help with the transition, but when they left, the inevitable happened. I was sad and lonely. There were no plans for every night. There were no friends down the hall or down the street. I had no social life to speak of. Since I was not going to school or work there, how would I ever make friends? What was there even to do in Delaware? Well, I wasn't old enough to go to the casino, which was really the only social atmosphere I was aware of. There was a mall nearby, but what fun is that alone? I honestly don't know what I did for those two weeks other than sit in front of my computer and sneak in another day trip back to New Jersey. There really wasn't much in the way of social media to speak of at the time. All I had at the time was an online messenger and some old version of a blog site. Though I can say, that began my first blogging experience. Little did I know where it would eventually take me! Somehow, I got through the two weeks in "my" new house and now it was time to head to college!

For most of my life, it was expected that I would choose a career doing something with animals. I always had a lot of pets and spent much of my childhood weekends at 4-H shows. When it came time to choose a college, I only looked at schools with animal programs. Since I was not entirely sure what I wanted to do with the rest of my life, I chose a school in Massachusetts that offered a Veterinary Science degree. With this degree, I could decide later where it would take me. It seemed as though I would have endless opportunities. I must admit that I did not really know what to expect, especially when I was basically deciding the rest of my life at only seventeen years old (the career part anyway). All I knew was it seemed like the right fit. The school was in a very small town and only had two hundred people living on campus. I should mention that at the time, it was also roughly 75% female populated. I went from a high school class of five hundred, to a campus of two hundred. It was a big change and not exactly what I expected from the college experience! Everyone knew everyone and there were not many guys!

My college years were honestly not all that exciting, as I could not wait to "start my life." Don't get me wrong, I had some great times with some great friends, but spent a lot of time working and studying. (That's what you're supposed to do, right?) I really do not have much of the "wild, crazy parties" and "insane drunken nights" to speak of. Well, maybe a few. The movie nights with friends and trips to the snack bar at night stick out in my mind more than the foam parties at frat houses and nights of sheer stupidity. I did date a few guys throughout this time, both on campus and off, long distance and nearby, but no serious boyfriends or anyone to write home about. I hadn't met my match, but I certainly had some fun along the way!

Ultimately, when it came down to it, the most important things I learned in college didn't come from any textbook or lab. I came out of the experience learning a lot about responsibility and friendship. When graduation came, it was time for everyone to move on and figure out what they were doing with their lives. I can't really explain how I figured everything out. I was not sure where I wanted to go or what I ultimately wanted to do. I knew that I really did not want to live in Delaware, and could not really afford to move back to New Jersey on my own. I had the opportunity to stay where I was and accepted a position right there at my college. This was not a paying job, but I would not have to worry about finding an apartment or paying rent. I would just move downstairs into an apartment, inside the dorm, and be able to live for free. I was also very excited to stay near one of my closest friends, and her daughter. I still needed to find an actual paying job. I ultimately chose a job that was not the appropriate fit. The Veterinary field does not come chock full of high paying jobs. Being somewhat of a closet science nerd, I accepted a position at a nearby research facility. And there it was, this part of my life had been figured out! Or so I thought.

I don't really like expressions, but this seems appropriate. "Nothing in life is ever as it seems." I never really considered myself to be optimistic or pessimistic, just a realist, but I was very optimistic about starting a new journey. As it turned out, I was wrong. As the school year progressed, I became more and more miserable. Once I got settled into my job, I realized this was not what I wanted. Although necessary, it was not something I wanted to be a part of. I dreaded getting up in the morning and driving there. Even more, I dreaded the entire day. As far as my second job was concerned, I was never very good at it. I would come home from work at night, tired and depressed, and have to deal with typical college student antics. It had only been a few years since I was a college freshman, and I do realize that I did the same things! Still, I have always felt old for my age, and this really did it. I was too old, or too mentally old, to be living in a dorm, staff member or not. I did not want to deal with running, screaming, and water balloon fights in the halls. I felt like I just couldn't win in either job. I tried to do my best, but I was too unhappy.

The negative quickly outweighed the positive. My life was not complete and it was time for a change. I can partially say "on a whim," though I did really think it through, I moved back to New Jersey. I knew things would never be truly the same as they used to be, but my gut told me I would find my happiness there. It was hard leaving the people behind that I truly loved in Massachusetts! Still, I knew this was the right choice. I took a job at a marketing company, which is where I met the man who would become my first true love, Alex. Though for roughly the first five months, we only walked past each other and had very limited work-related interactions, one day everything changed. Like a whirlwind, he swept me off my feet, married me, and we began our life together. After a short stay there, I went back into my real career and was hired as a Veterinary Technician at a small nearby animal hospital. Though not exactly a prime salary, it was what I really wanted to be doing. We bought a house and settled down in our home state of New Jersey.

Like any marriage, we had our ups and downs. I can honestly say we were deeply and madly in love. We both made mistakes, just like anyone else. We suffered through financial struggles and something even more traumatic, infertility. Those were our two major sources of difficulty. Money is typically the number one thing which couples fight about, and we certainly did. Infertility, pregnancy loss, and financial struggle are huge factors in many divorces. Still, we survived both, and a very high-risk pregnancy before the birth of our beautiful daughter, Alexa. Though at times life was difficult, we still made it through. I liked to say that we fought hard, but we loved hard too. Looking back on our marriage truly has taught me a lot. There are certainly things I wish I could change, but all I can do is learn from my mistakes and move on.

I can say that most of our problems were financial or circumstantial but, in being true to myself, I admit our main downfall was communication. I'll be the first to say that I missed all the signs of mental illness. I just didn't know! Instead of pushing him to get help, I would tell him he was acting childish and needed to be an adult about things. Was he just acting childish or was it a sign of things? I really don't know. Well, maybe I do and I just won't admit it yet. Day after day, he would self-diagnose something new for his behavior. The ones that stick out most in my mind are ADHD and symptoms resulting from a past head injury. When he was officially diagnosed with depression, he denied it and moved on. I can look back and say, ideally I should have pushed the issue further. When it comes to a relationship, you choose your battles. As difficult as it is to admit now, there was a lot going wrong and a lot of red flags. Looking back, I believe I was choosing not to see them. We were both working full-time and exhausted with a new baby. Through hard times, we always seemed to snap right back from an incident and go back to our happy life. Being the closest person to Alex, I believed that I truly knew everything there was to know about him. In reality, there was no way I could have ever fully known what was going on in his head. I believe he wasn't even sure himself.

Recently, I was called a spitfire. Maybe I am too blunt and honest. Obviously, if I am writing this, I am a very open person. Alex was much more introverted and quiet, except when you got him dancing or laughing. Our personalities and communication styles were very different, but we complemented each other well. He was truly an amazing man. He loved me and wanted me to be happy. I can't help but think if we had all the information needed and understood what he was going through, the outcome may have been different. Maybe not, but I can't help but wonder.

This brings me to situations surrounding his death. When I met Alex, everyone told me that he would get obsessed with a hobby. He would want to be the best at it, spend a ton of money on it, and actually become the best. Then, he would forget all about it, and move on to something else. Boy, was this true! When it was the Rubik's cube, he had to have every single one ever made! They were specially ordered from Germany, different colors, different sizes, etc. No big deal, that hobby wasn't too expensive. Still to this day, I am in awe of his ability to solve one in seconds.

When his new endeavor was cycling, that got really expensive! It certainly got a little out of control, but it was a healthy hobby, right? I even tried to get into it! I got my own road bike, equipment, tight cycling shorts, and everything! I was very proud of Alex's fundraisers and crazy long bike rides. Still, I felt I was not cut out for cycling. The fitness interest even expanded to running with expensive barefoot sneakers, swimming, and more! Like the last one, these hobbies, of course, faded as well.

Photography was the next a big one! Now that's an even more expensive hobby! He always needed a new lens, bag, flash, computer, or editing program. The list goes on. However, I decided to turn this interest into a business, so it would literally pay for itself. Alex was so incredibly talented! We had a lot of memorable times pursuing this dream and our new business together. Many of our weekends were spent doing photo shoots for friends, family, and new clients.

You get the idea. When the next hobby was guns, I was NOT about to jump on board. I admittedly am not comfortable with them, especially with a baby in the house. I take responsibility for having my own fears and opinions on them. I am, in no way, anti-gun. I believe in the right to bear arms. I believe it is an appropriate choice for some people, but not for me. There was no agreeing on this. I firmly believe that something of this magnitude should be agreed to in a marriage. But what happens when you cannot find a common ground? For me, we had been married for years and he had never shown an interest in firearms. He had never been exposed to them, until moving to a state where they were much more prominent and more importantly, legal. It had never been a topic for discussion prior. Yet at this point, he was 100% fighting me that "guns are safe." I had to hear the "guns are safe" talk EVERY SINGLE NIGHT. Finally, I agreed to one gun, to be kept in a safe, away from Alexa. I did not agree to any other financial (or otherwise) obligation in the gun department. I should have known this was not the end.

Now comes the financial aspect of our life together. I guess blind trust was a bad idea. He took care of the bills. I knew they were getting paid. I told him what I needed to spend, and he told me what I could spend. I was always under the impression that we were just barely making ends meet. I had payment plans for medical bills and couldn't always afford to fill my truck with gas. We agreed that all purchases were to be discussed with the other partner. It was rare that we didn't agree and even further, never seemed to have a reason not to trust the other person.

In days before his death, I logged into my bank account. I never do this. I never felt the need. Something as simple as a co-worker wondering if our direct deposit had gone through on the holiday opened up a world of disbelief. I immediately discovered charges to a gun shop and just as quickly, called him out on it. These were not charges I had agreed to. Nor, did I agree to furthering the hobby. This opened up some arguing. But still, we managed to have a great weekend together.

It was not until the morning of his death that he just started to admit everything. He left for work and the texts began. He admitted to having two guns (really he had six, which I still would not fully discover for almost three years). He also admitted to taking out thousands of dollars in credit cards behind my back. He had spent unimaginable amounts of money at the gun range, and repeatedly went there behind my back. I had been under the impression his job had paid for his gun license, but really, it had come out of our paychecks. He said he knew that he was a compulsive liar and throughout our relationship had lied about money more times than he could count, even stating it was quite possibly thousands of times. He had me basically living in poverty, while spending the majority of what we had behind my back.

I know what you're thinking. How could I keep saying he was such an incredible person, while at the same time exposing some extreme faults? Yes, there was a dark side of him I had never known until this point. I could say, nobody's perfect, which is true. However, I do not believe any of this was done with rational thinking. The REAL Alex was the kind, loving, fun, sweet man I had married.

He kept apologizing, and asking me not to leave him. He kept saying he regretted it and calling me the love of his life. He kept saying he doesn't know why he does this and wants to stop, but doesn't know how. Even further, that things like this had gone on his entire adult life. Spend, regret, spend, regret, spend, regret. This was his pattern, and I had no idea. Many of us have this pattern, and I would not label it as a disorder, but this was extreme! Later on, I would find out that in the past, he had gone on extreme spending sprees, never even opening the boxes. The items just piled up at work and never even came home.

That day, he sent me all his credit card logins and

promised to sell everything he could. We agreed I would take over the finances. I asked him to promise me that everything would be okay, and we would move on to resolve this however we had to. His one stipulation was he needed to be allowed to smoke. It was never that he was not "allowed." I had quit smoking and asked for the courtesy of him not smoking around me or our baby.

Alex did say he thought "killing himself" was a better option, feeling that I would be better off without him and his debt. I told him that was not a solution and that losing him would ruin my life. He said he was going crazy from guilt, that he was hurting and stressed. He said it was a fleeting thought, and he was not serious.

I said I had no intentions of leaving him. I truly didn't have intentions of leaving. Though I would never say that I disagree with divorce, I still wanted to hold my promise. I still believed we were meant to be together. Admittedly, I was very angry and still believe I had every right to be. I knew and promised I would try my absolute best to forgive him. I'm not good at holding grudges anyway. Looking back now, I'm not sure he never ACTUALLY said he wouldn't hurt himself, but it certainly did seem implied.

Taking a step back, I feel I should mention another pattern in his behavior. Excuse my language, but he often talked out of his ass! Again, he was not great at expressing himself. He was not as articulate as I tend to be. He's said a lot of absolutely ridiculous things that ultimately had no real meaning and would later say he either had no idea why he said those things, or had no recollection of the conversation. I believed his mention of suicide was just that.

Interestingly enough, that evening was New Year's Eve. I was at my parents' house STILL texting with Alex. He said he was driving from work and would meet me there. With everything that went on that day, I still had hopes of a pleasant evening. I was stressed, and hoped it would just be dropped so we could move forward. I was feeding Alexa her dinner. Time passed. He was late and his texts stopped. His final text to me said, "I love you and Alexa."

I texted him over and over. I called him over and over. I began to worry, and then progressed to utter panic. I drove the half-mile to our house, hoping maybe he went home to change. The garage door was open and dark, but his car was right there, in his spot, as if warning me that something was terribly wrong. The house was completely dark. I threw open my truck door, left it open, and ran in the house, screaming for him. He did not answer. I saw the basement light was on. I opened the door and screamed for him, but there was no answer.

I heard music. To this day, I wish I could remember what was playing. I smelled cigarette smoke, coming up from downstairs. He's smoking in the house?! I ran down the stairs as quickly as I could, somehow knowing what I would find. There he was. I was right. Forever burned in my brain is the image of him under his workout bench, foot caught up above, gun on the floor in the distance, and laying in a large pool of blood. There was a wooden stool nearby. His phone, glasses, lighter, and half full pack of cigarettes sat there. There were five cigarette butts put out on the floor. He had a half an hour, at least, to tell me what was going on, or call a friend or a suicide hotline. Sadly, he didn't.

For a split second, I actually thought I could scream at him, "What is wrong with you?" and he would get up and say, "Oops. Sorry. That was stupid. Never mind." I ran up the stairs and back down just as fast. I called 911. I can still hear the 911 call in my head:

"911 what is your emergency?"

"My husband killed himself."

"What?"

"I just got home and found my husband shot in the head."

They asked if I wanted to do CPR and I said yes. Somehow, I managed to move a 250 pound man and start. I texted my parents "HELP 911," between breaths and chest compressions. The 911 operator finally said EMS was in the house and I screamed and screamed for them for what felt like forever, until they came down the stairs and found us. They took over and I ran outside. I laid on the floor of my garage, and even as a non-smoker, I began to chain smoke. I clearly remember my dad's truck pulling up, him jumping out, putting his coat on me, and sitting down on the floor next to me. It was only minutes until they came to tell us that Alex was gone. The wording didn't even make sense to me. "There is brain matter on the floor, which is not conducive to life."

EMS began to check on me, concerned with my state of mind and my blood pressure. I had just found my husband had died, and began to chain smoke. Of course my blood pressure was up! Soon, a detective came in and critically asked me if we had been physically fighting. I was unaware that my face was completely covered in blood. I wouldn't discover this until walking into the hospital bathroom that evening, and coming face-to-face with a mirror.

Not long after being prescribed anti-anxiety medication, it was time for my interrogation. I had watched police shows before and thought I had the basic idea of how this would go. The questions seemed ridiculous.

"Did he eat breakfast?"
"I made him a protein shake."
"Did he ACTUALLY drink it?"
"I have no idea! He left the house with it."

"Where did you get married?"
"What were his hobbies?"
"What were you fighting about?"
"Where did you think he was?"

"Was he left handed or right handed?"

"Was the gun in his hand?"

"Had he ever cheated on you?"

It was at this point that my dad yelled, "That's enough!" and walked out. I defended the detective stating this was his job and he had to ask me these things. That may have bothered me in a normal situation, but I certainly wasn't my normal self.

The officer then went on to say they had already read our texts from the day. (OMG Alex had a habit of sending bathroom photos to me and just had the night before! Did they see that?) The officer asked if I could unlock his phone for them again. I could not. Alex had shown me that damn swipe password so many times and I still couldn't remember it! They apologized for my loss, asked if they could call anyone, and explained it was (especially considering the texts they read) clearly suicide.

Months later, when they finally returned his phone and gun, the detective told my dad, "Alex was a great guy, something just went wrong." I'm not sure why, but I truly found some peace in that statement.

Well, there it is. In a matter of moments, I became a young widow, a single mom, and a survivor of suicide. The rest of the evening and days to come were such a blur. I have moments of vivid recollection and other periods of time that just seem to be missing. Like images laying on a cutting room floor, I see myself in various stages throughout that week. That day is a complete blur and can honestly say that, after finding him, I was no longer mentally able to grasp the concept of what had happened. I couldn't feel anything. I couldn't understand anything. I couldn't scream. I couldn't cry. I was just numb, as if watching myself as an outsider. It wasn't me at all. It would not become "real" for a while. I'm still not sure I could pinpoint the exact moment it did.

What I do know is I woke up the next morning at my parents' house to the blunt realization that this was not a nightmare. It DID happen, even though it was all still so surreal. What did I do for the six days until the funeral? I can only imagine I just stumbled around. I did not eat for days. It was a new year, and I was starting it by scrubbing my blood-stained skin and calling friends and family with the horrible news.

The initial reaction was, of course, shock. Upon hearing the news, one of the top responses I got from people was, "Were you fighting?" Automatically, I felt that they were trying to blame me. Well, yes, as I explained earlier, we were fighting that day. Actually, not as much fighting as I was angry and he was sorry. But for the sake of argument, (pun intended) let's go with fighting. Do you fight with your spouse? Of course you do! How many times had we fought in six years? Why was this time different? I maintain that I had every right to be angry that day, but that does not make this hurt any less. In fact, I believe it made it hurt even more.

As time went on, friends and family began to arrive for support, to help with my child, and to celebrate Alex's life, some not even really knowing what had happened. I planned a funeral to the best of my ability. I picked out my favorite clothes to bury him in and decided on the graveyard, casket, and services. I never imagined having to make such awful decisions, especially at this point in my life. Was I even doing what he wanted?

Six days after his death, we celebrated his life with, what I would consider, a rather traditional funeral. The night before, I had my own private viewing. My parents, one very close friend, and I were the only ones in attendance. I remember being in a fog walking into the building. It still wasn't real. I took a deep breath, walked in, and came face-to-face with a large beautiful canvas of his portrait. Suddenly, the pain became unbearable. There he was, exactly as I remembered him. I attempted to regain some composure and was instructed that as I walked into the next room, I would turn right and walk all the way through to the casket. I remember the first sight of it, but can't remember how quickly I walked up to it. The rest is very much a blur. I screamed, I cried, and I talked to him. I asked for a step stool to get closer to him. I held his hand and stroked his hair, before I was asked not to. I practically climbed in there with him. I cried on his chest, leaving tear stains on my favorite sweater vest that I decided to bury him in. I finally understood what people meant when they go to a funeral and say, "He looked so good." He looked like the Alex I knew and loved. Besides being dead, you would never know he had been shot. I held his foot. His ice cold body felt good on my migraine-ridden head. I can still close my eyes and almost feel the the moment I laid my head on him. I even took photos of him. I still don't know why. I just can't explain it. I can't remember any of what I said to him. It was probably along the lines of "How am I supposed to live without you?" and "It wasn't supposed to be this way." I've been told that most of my speaking was incoherent through the tears, but one quote that deeply resonated with me years later is, "Why did you do this and why didn't you let me help you?" I left there knowing the horror the next day would bring. The next morning, a limo would be waiting to take me to my husband's funeral. I was twenty-eight years old, married for only four years, and just had a baby. How could this be happening to me? Well, it did.

Somehow, I survived those days and vowed that I would continue. I had been pushed, kicking and screaming, into a life I did not want! A life of widowhood. I had a seven-month-old daughter and I decided then that I would not die with him. I would give Alexa the life she deserves, even with having such an unfair start. She only had one parent now, and she needed me. The next day, everything was done. The funeral was over. His body was laid to rest. Everyone was leaving, and I was somehow starting my new life.

In the weeks to come, sometimes I was amazed that I was able to get out of bed, get dressed, and function. So maybe I was wearing track pants and a t-shirt, and I'm sure hadn't showered in two days or more, but still, I was standing, I was walking, eating, drinking, and going to work. I was taking care of my daughter and doing the things I HAD to do. I explained it by saying, I don't have a choice. My husband chose death, and I chose life. Although I had only been existing at the time, I still chose life.

I started this journey not knowing how to live without him. The truth is, I didn't. I always knew that I physically could, but what about mentally? My husband, partner in life, love of my life, and father of my child was gone. He was not coming back, no matter how much I wanted him to, and even if he wanted to. Do I even need to mention again that he chose this! That was a lot to swallow when I woke up every morning to the same nightmare that was my life. I always wondered how people go on after a major life-altering tragedy. Here's the answer. You just do. The baby needs a mother, the pets need to be cared for, the bills need to be paid, and I was left to do it, so I did.

I needed a way to heal, to grieve, to get the demons out of my head, and to make something positive from the trauma I'd been handed. That was the start of my blog, The Widow Next Door.

Disclaimer:

The following blog was not written by an experienced author. The posts were written in real-time by me, an emotionally-crazed woman basically scribbling out the madness in my mind. They were meant to reflect my mindset during this very tragic time in my life.

◆◆◆

February 2013

Tuesday, February 12th, 2013 at 10:40 pm
My First Support Group

State Police Victim Services referred me to a support group called "Survivors of Suicide" (SOS). To start with, I sort of have an issue with the name of the group. I did not personally *survive* suicide. I am not the one attempting suicide. I am the survivor/family member of someone who actually succeeded at taking their own life. How do you properly and respectfully put that into words, without it sounding so awful? I don't really know. Nothing is "not-awful" about this. So, I decided this group would help me.

It was 1/31/13, exactly one month after his death, to the day. Apparently, this was a new group because there were only three of us and the moderator. All of them had lost their sons to suicide. Not quite the same life as I was living! These women were much further along in the grieving process than I was and told me all kinds of stories of what was in store for me. I felt horrible! I did not want to think about being miserable in 5-10 years from now. They told me how you are in shock during the first year and the second year is worse. I was looking for hope, not horror stories of

first, second, and third holidays. Still staying at my parents'
house, I went "home," feeling lost and alone. This is not what I
was looking for!

What I can say is, I was sent home with an SOS handbook
(there's that term again) and it made the night (and hour drive)
worthwhile. It truly *has* helped. Has it erased any of my pain? No,
I can't say it has, but maybe explained a few things. I did learn a
lot about the history and stigma of suicide. That may have opened
my eyes a bit. I was told to try the group at least four times before
deciding if it is right for me. I may try another meeting place that
is busier, in hopes to find people that may understand my specific
situation a little better. We'll see.

Wednesday, February 13th, 2013 at 12:21 am
Rings

Something that came along with all of this mess were
thoughts that I felt I should not even be worrying about, but just
couldn't help it. One thing that was always on my mind was my
rings. I wasn't actually married anymore, so should I be wearing
them? I mean, you do say "Till death do you part."

At first, I couldn't bear the thought of taking them off.
They were a part of our marriage and life together. I couldn't part
with that. I never wore my real rings to work, so I told myself
when I went back after a few weeks, that would be the time. Well
the time came, and I just couldn't do it. The strange thing is, I
started to feel stupid wearing them! Almost as if, as a single
woman, I had no right. It was an internal struggle that really, in
the scheme of things, I shouldn't have had to worry about.

Finally, amidst changing diapers, doing dishes, cleaning
etc., I realized I needed to take them off like I would normally do
anyway. I put them on a necklace and they have stayed there ever

since. I wear his wedding band on my thumb, which I have worn since they gave it to me at the funeral. I also wear a promise ring he got me when we started dating. My left ring finger remains empty. It feels weird, but it feels like the rest of my life does.

The answer to all this is: it is different for everyone and I think each person knows when the time is right. I won't be ready to move on for a long time, but this was the first step to starting a life that is "mine," not "ours."

Wednesday, February 13th, 2013 at 2:02 am
He Was a Good Man

I constantly feel the need to defend him. Every time I find myself telling someone what happened, I always have the urge to say, "But he was a wonderful person, a great father, and loved us so much." Why do I do that? The only thing I can really say is he really was all those things! He was a wonderful husband and father. He did love us very much. He was very talented, worked very hard, and was a happy, caring person.

I don't want people to remember him for the one bad day in his life. I don't want people to remember him for one huge mistake. I want people to remember how he was alive, not how he died. I want to remember his smile and his warmth. I want hear his laugh and hear him call me "Mowface." I want to picture him playing with his daughter, not the way I found him. I want everyone to do the same.

We all know there is a huge negativity associated with someone who takes their own life. Don't look at him that way. Look at him as the man we knew and loved. He was that man. The man that took his life was not "him."

Wednesday, February 13th, 2013 at 11:38 am
Questions

When facing an unexpected death of a loved one, you are left with so many unanswered questions. Most importantly, for me, was why? Why would he do this? In the past few weeks after his death, I have certainly put a lot of pieces together and at least created a version of my own answer to why.

I have talked to his friends and family, reread our texts from that day, talked to my therapist, gotten insight from his co-workers, gone through his effects from work, looked into aspects of his life I was not a part of, and found things I was unaware of in my house. I'll admit, I have even tried talking to him at the place of his death and gotten help from a psychic. I have always believed in being able to contact the spirit world and this has helped.

Details on this can be a post of its own, but with all of this, I still wish he could stand here and explain it all to me. What was he thinking at that moment? Could he really think this was better for me? When did he make the final decision? Why did he use a gun, knowing how I felt about guns?

Then the morbid questions arise. Did it hurt? How long was it before I got there? What if I had gotten there sooner? Why in the basement? Didn't he realize I would find him and what that would do to me? Now, I know in my head that I am not to blame, but my heart still asks, what should I have said differently? What should I have done differently? Why didn't I realize? How was I so stupid as to not catch on that his last text said he loves me? To take that further, what was the last text he saw from me? Ultimately, what could I have done to change this? I would have done anything to save him, if only I had known.

Thursday, February 14th, 2013 at 2:30 pm
Valentine's Day

This is my first Valentine's Day alone in six years. I'm not actually alone. I have my beautiful baby girl to be my Valentine. My beautiful, coughing, runny-nosed, miserable, crying baby girl, who has, somehow, been sleeping for the past five minutes. Today, I am going to take my daughter to the pediatrician, bring flowers to the man I love (which he would probably think is stupid), do some online shopping, probably order a pizza, and eat dinner alone. It is 9:30 am and I am already feeling so loved with the amount of friends and family thinking of me today. I will admit, I'm cranky today, but I will keep reminding myself, it's just another day!

Thursday, February 14th, 2013 at 8:02 pm
Maybe Today Isn't "Just Another Day"

I can't help but wonder if I should take back my comment that Valentine's day is "just another day." Everywhere I turn, reminders of Alex smack me in the face. First, Facebook had a huge banner with his face, reminding me to buy something for my Valentine, UGH. That made me gasp with shock. I X'ed it out and moved on. I had to take Alexa to the doctor. They asked that I take her to the outpatient services at the hospital (where he used to work) for a test. As soon as I pulled in the parking lot, I was faced with his exact blue Chevy Aveo in the lot he used to park in. COME ON! Of course, I had to pass it four times while trying to find a spot in that madhouse of a parking lot.

After arguing with them over insurance, I was sent to an outside diagnostic lab. I walked up to the door to come face-to-face with a large photo of a gun with a slash through it, noting that guns were not allowed in there. Obviously, that is always there, but seeing it for the first time freaked me out. It worked out, and we were on our way.

I knew better than to go through the McDonald's drive-thru (ew), but I was hungry and trying to avoid taking Alexa out of the car again. I was sitting in the drive-thru line and Alex's co-worker walked right in front of my car. Wow, what are the chances of that? After a quick trip to the graveyard, it was time to go home for the day. And, Facebook strikes again. I'm kicking myself for not saving the photo, but I was freaked out and immediately refreshed the page. The ad on the side of the page was a man holding a camera (like a camera Alex used) with the long lens to the side of his head (like a gun). His eyes were squeezed shut as if he was about to push the shutter button (trigger). I've had enough today!

Friday, February 15th, 2013 at 11:39 am
Are You Okay?

I am incredibly grateful for the outpouring of generosity and caring from the people around me. It is just amazing the number of people I have been in contact with over the past few weeks. It is nice to know that people care. What everyone wants to know is "How are you?" I never know how to answer that. Are they looking for me to say "I'm great!" Well, clearly, I'm not. Are they looking for my innermost thoughts? Probably not.

I feel the urge to say "I'm fine." In the general sense of the term, I'm not. When I hear the word fine, I always think of the joke that it stands for "Fucked up, insecure, neurotic, emotional." That sounds about right! All in all, I usually go with "okay." I am "okay." I am not in a puddle on the floor, for the moment. I'm not in a screaming fit of rage, for the moment. I am sitting/standing here talking/texting with you, for the moment.

Saturday, February 16th, 2013 at 11:57 pm
While Mourning...

Life doesn't stop moving just because you are in mourning. As I mentioned in earlier posts, Alexa is sick. Yesterday, she tested positive for RSV. Normally, this does not mean too much, but in an infant (especially a preemie), it can be serious. Like any parent, I feel so helpless and so bad for her. My stress is through the roof! We have added nebulizer treatments and antibiotics to our daily regimen and hopefully all will be well for her soon. Here is the real kicker. I fought for months to get her the RSV vaccine, but insurance refused to cover it. They will only cover babies born eight weeks early, and Alexa was born seven weeks and one day early.

Now here we are. Alexa has RSV. Even better, I have been going back and forth with insurance companies for weeks trying to figure out if she is covered and, if not, who is going to cover her. She was on Alex's insurance. First, they say she isn't covered. Then, they say she still is. Well, when I actually need the insurance, it is DENIED! Okay, don't panic, I'll get it all figured out. All of this will only cost, thousands? Can't do anything about it over the weekend.

Now, to figure out her medications. Walmart sent home a bottle of powder. THEY SENT HOME A BOTTLE OF POWDER!? Come on! Back out in the snow to have them actually mix up the medication and give me a dosing syringe. Really? Their response was, "Hmm yeah, we are supposed to mix that before sending it home." Ya think?

Moral of the story: The normal stressors of life do not stop just because you are in mourning.

Sunday, February 17th, 2013 at 12:22 pm
Gravestone

A big decision looming overhead is choosing the gravestone. I met with the designer to give him my ideas and received some drawings and computer generated photos a few weeks later. I was excited to receive the ideas because I feel that when the headstone is finally up, it will give me some sense of closure. I stared at the photos for what felt like hours and just could not decide. I got input from others. Could I justify spending the extra money for a special design? It's just a headstone. No amount of money spent will bring him back. Still, it had to be something I liked and was comfortable with.

I was told to sleep on it. I did and it drove me nuts the entire next day! I need to decide so all this can be over! I finally picked one, but knew I wanted to make some changes to it. We let the designer know that I was still thinking, and that I may want to make some changes, but I was happy with the designs. He let us know that he had another idea he would like to show me. Sure, just as I had some things figured out, here comes a curveball. I was stressing while waiting for the new design. Days went on and I forgot for a little while. Obviously, I have a lot of other things going on. What brought this back up? I was walking down the street at lunch yesterday, when a huge Tombstone pizza truck drove by with the saying on it, "What do you want on your tombstone?" Ugh…

Sunday, February 17th, 2013 at 2:04 pm
Social Anxiety

I have to admit, with everything going on, I have been getting a little bit of social anxiety. Anyone who knows me well knows that this isn't me. I have the constant fear of saying something inappropriate, doing something stupid in my "autopilot haze," or crying on the floor of a store. Yes, I *did* actually cry on the floor of Toys R Us. Does it get better?

Monday, February 18th, 2013 at 10:58 pm
Strength

So many people marvel at how strong I am, tell me that I'm stronger than they are and one of the strongest people they know. Six years ago today was one of the best days of my life. Alex and I got engaged. Today was one of my worst days.

I started the day waking up from numerous dreams of him last night, to realize that, sadly, they were dreams and this was still my life. Upon realizing the date, I cried my eyes out while trying to get ready for work. Through the day, I argued with two different insurance companies and I'm still left with a sick baby and no insurance. Have I mentioned I'm sick too?

Today, I am physically, emotionally, and mentally drained.

Tuesday, February 19th, 2013 at 12:57 pm
Cliché

Not long after going back to work, someone at work said, "Whatever doesn't kill you, only makes you stronger." Now this was not directed at me, but still, I said, "Well, I'm not dead and I'm certainly not strong." His answer was, "I didn't give it a time limit." I didn't know how to respond to that. I think about what he said all the time. It's true. Sometimes I backslide, but I hope to get a little stronger every day.

Wednesday, February 20th, 2013 at 4:31 pm
Sometimes, It's Just Too Much!

Sometimes, It's just too much! I have been on antibiotics for ten days and I am still sick. I went to the doctor again yesterday and of course was put in the room where Alex and I were when our doctor told him he had depression. Thankfully, I had so much else going on in my mind, I did not have a chance to really let it upset me. I was told I either have Bronchitis or Walking Pneumonia and need to start nebulizers and steroids. Great! That's just what I need right now. I drove to the hospital for a chest x-ray, then to the lab for bloodwork, and got home just in time to get Alexa ready and take her to her pediatrician. Thankfully, she is doing better.

Then, we went to the chiropractor. On the way home, we stopped for formula and her medicine. I got home, made her bottle, got her settled and went to start my nebulizer. My mind kept telling me, "I'm forgetting something, I'm forgetting something," the steroid! I called the doctor's office. Yup, I left the Rx on the counter. Well, can't expect me to remember everything right now, can I? They offered to call it in, and that is fixed.

Now, to deal with Alexa's continuing insurance issue. I was told they are legally required to inform the policyholder that the policy is ending. Since the policyholder is deceased, they are under no obligation to let me know that my child's insurance is ending! They had no answer to the fact that every document they sent me has a different date of effect. They are also allowed to cancel her insurance as of the date of his death. There does NOT have to be a waiting period. Awesome!

So, I tried calling MY insurance again. They still did not have an answer for me, but they were trying to help. They were unable to add her in the system because they only allow you to add a child to insurance within thirty days of the "change of life."

But, because her insurance company was (excuse my language) fucking around and would not give me the paperwork I needed within that time period, they were going to try to override this. There was nothing else I could do with this for the day.

Thankfully, my mom offered to pick up my medication so I didn't have to go back out. She got there, and it wasn't ready. Why is it not ready? Insurance denied it. Why did insurance deny it? They only allow you to take 1.4 tablets of Prednisone and my first dose is two tablets. Seriously? How do you even cut 1.4 tablets? Whatever, Prednisone is cheap and I need it.

I spent most of the night tossing and turning and trying to sleep. Really, I spent most of the night coughing. I did not have enough time between coughs to attempt to sleep. Every time I would finally fall asleep, I'd wake up to pee. Of course, I had just taken 20mg of Prednisone and had about three cups of tea so that sounds about right. When morning came, I was a mess. Sick baby, sick mommy, dogs need to go out, baby needs food and medicine and nebulizer, parents need to get to work, etc. My mind was racing. My cough was worse, and I was exhausted. And Alex should be here to help me! I'm at the end of my sanity rope and trying to slowly crawl back up.

Thursday, February 21st, 2013 at 6:25 pm
Good News!

Alexa has insurance! No thanks to the idiots at her insurance company, but mine was able to add her to my policy and even back-date it! So thankful for them!

I do not have Pneumonia! I just have Bronchitis. I still feel like crap, but I'd rather have Bronchitis.

I got the new gravestone design and with one minor change, it will be perfect!

With all that off my shoulders, I really miss him today. I actually have the chance to just miss him right now. I want to hug him and feel his warmth. I want to smell him and hear his voice. I want a text that says "Mow." I want to hold his hand. I really want to see him smile. I hope someday I don't miss those things as much.

Friday, February 22nd, 2013 at 2:26 am
Racing Mind

Trying to go to bed at night is when my mind begins to race. I sometimes start by replaying the night of his death and bounce all over the place. Here it goes:

- picture him lying there where I found him
- wonder why again
- get angry
- replay old conversations (good and bad)
- daydream about him still being here
- laugh about some fun times
- try to fix things in my head
- write blog posts in my head that will never happen
- think of ideas of my book that I wont remember in the morning
- miss my cats and think about moving home
- worry about living "alone"
- do some financial planning
- worry about Alexa growing up without a dad
- daydream about being happy again someday (yeah right)
- think back to things and wonder how I missed that!

- get sad
- get mad again
- try to picture him smiling
- try to hear his voice (I have a hard time with this)
- make sure I remember where the spot on his hand and face were
- feel how cold he was laying on him in the casket
- wonder when I could turn back the clock to to fix this
- think about the gravestone
- wonder where he is now
- wonder if he can see me
- daydream about conversations that will never happen
- ask him questions and actually expect answers
- stress over the "unknown"
- realize I'm hungry and have to pee and debate getting up Does this ever end?

Monday, February 25th, 2013 at 4:46 am
Sunday

I woke up today to the sounds of my little girl talking to herself down the hall. I went in her room to see that beautiful smiling face. It's always a good way to start the day. It was not long after that my migraine hit. Great, just what I need. I have a lot planned for today. I have dealt with migraines for as long as I can remember. I even have memories of having them as a child, though at the time, I didn't know what they were.

Medication and a nap didn't help. Thankfully, a few cups of coffee did and I was back to my day. I spent some time at my house getting things done. It doesn't feel like home there anymore, but I do feel like I'm getting more comfortable there. I cleaned up the smashed vase (thank you kitties) and grabbed some random things I needed. Then, onto litterboxes. After dumping them all out, I realized I had no litter! Well, let's just say I'm lucky I didn't end up on "people of Walmart". I sure look like trash. Well, who knows, maybe I did. I haven't checked. I'm sure I looked crazy enough buying five boxes of litter, cat food, Oreos, cough drops, and cigarettes anyway.

I got that all taken care of, showered, dressed, and did my usual Sunday trip to the graveyard. I even told Alexa I was going to see daddy. She doesn't understand anyway. I always want to go, but when I get there, I never know what to do there. I cleaned up the grave a little and rearranged the little gifts I bring him. I brought some Easter egg things today.

As I've mentioned, there is no gravestone yet. There is just a photo of him staked into the ground. I stare and stare at it in disbelief as he smiles back at me. I know all this happened and I know it's real, I lived it. Or do I? Sometimes it is just surreal. How can this actually be my husband's grave? Nah, I'm going to see him again soon. We are still together. Life is normal. I almost can convince myself sometimes.

It's cold and I had nothing more to do there really. I know it's not like he's actually there. I can talk to him anywhere. I had planned for weeks to go out to to dinner tonight with some friends from work. I have been sick so didn't 100% commit to it, but really wanted to go. As usual, the social anxiety began to kick in as I got ready. It would be easy to say I was too sick to go, but did I want that? Somehow, I forced myself through the anxiety, got dressed, drove the hour, and made my legs walk up to the building. I'm glad I did. I had a good time with great people and ate some amazing food. It was worth the anxiety. Now I'm alone and lonely and my princess is asleep. Hopefully I can get some sleep tonight too. I made it through today. Tomorrow is another day.

Tuesday, February 26th, 2013 at 12:41 am
Some Thoughts

I have an amazing support system. My parents spend most of their time helping me with my life and my daughter. My friends (although most are far away) go out of their way to do whatever they can for me. My job has been amazing. I get to go to a place almost every day where I am surrounded by people who care about me. There are even those who care that I never expected to. This blog has given me a chance to express my feelings and grief in a healthy way and give people a glimpse into what I am living.

People have reached out to tell me that they are amazed at how well I write. I don't know about that, but I just write what I feel and express myself honestly. Many have told me how it is helping them as well. I hope someday this blog can become even bigger. I want something good to come out of this horrible situation.

I hope to help others cope when they find themselves in similar situations to mine. I want people to learn about mental illness and suicide and have a better understanding of circumstances surrounding it. I have clearly expressed before that my husband was a wonderful and talented man. He should be regarded as such. A very select few people in my life seem to disagree with the path that I have chosen. I have been given the impression that it is felt that I should be ashamed and embarrassed of my life and my husband. I will not be. I love him and respect him and will continue to do so. His memory will be a good one. I have nothing to hide and I am here to help others and myself. I am not here to hurt anyone.

Tuesday, February 26th, 2013 at 11:57 am
Every Time Our Eyes Meet...

When it came time to pick our wedding song, I really wanted to dance to "Amazed" by Lonestar, but we just couldn't agree. We decided on "From This Moment" by Shania Twain, but said we would also be sure to dance to the other song later in the night. When that song came on, he was nowhere to be found. I was very disappointed. My cousin came to dance with me. I couldn't imagine dancing with anyone else at that moment. About a minute into the song, Alex came rushing to me on the dance floor to finish the dance with me. Anyone who knows him won't be surprised to hear that he was in the bathroom. This happened to us on two other occasions at other events. We always miss this song! He did finally admit to regretting not using it as our official wedding song.

I do believe in the spirit world and that spirits can walk among us. Someone told me that a sign that your loved one is around is when you are thinking of them and a song that reminds you of them comes on the radio. I spend a lot of time driving and a lot of time thinking of Alex. One day, "Amazed" came on the radio in the car. I hadn't heard it in years and cried my eyes out. Only two days later, I heard it again. This time I got angry. I started screaming at him. Yep, I was that crazy lady sitting in traffic screaming at no one in the car. "You left me! If you loved me so much you would still be here! How could you do this to me? I wanted to spend my whole life with you by my side!" Weeks have passed and I haven't heard the song again. I'm not sure how I feel about that.

Wednesday, February 27ᵗʰ, 2013 at 9:07 pm
Misery Loves Company

What a bunch of crap! I may be miserable, but I don't want to be. I want to spend my time around happy people. I want others in my life to be happy. I would like nothing more than to be a part of something special right now. I am a social butterfly at heart. I thrive on excitement and things to look forward to. I want to help someone plan their wedding or share in the joy of someone having a baby. I don't want to ever be the downer of a group. I want to be something, do something, and be important to people. I want to be the friend you go to for a laugh or a cry, not the person you have to walk on eggshells around. Share your joys with me. I will be happy for you. Ask me for advice. I may not be the best at it, but I will listen and will try. I admit, I am unhappy in life right now, but I have hope. I recently wrote about the simple things in life. I miss making Alex smile, but I can still make others smile, and I want to.

Thursday, February 28ᵗʰ, 2013 at 9:30 pm
Crying

I cried a lot today. Why today? I have no idea. I don't know what happened. I don't know what started it. I'm sad. Tears started and the next thing I knew I was hysterical and I just can't stop. I don't think I need to say that I miss him, but I will. I miss him! I'm usually one of those people that cries and you can't even tell. Not today! What a mess! I look like I've been crying for days! This won't be the last time. I can't be strong all the time.

March 2013

Sunday, March 3rd, 2013 at 2:11 am
Strange

Sometimes life feels so strange. I was excited to get some something in the mail today, so after work, I drove straight to my house to get it. Pulling onto my street, I suddenly felt so strange. It felt like I was heading home to Alex on a normal Saturday afternoon. It started to creep me out. I pulled in the driveway and walked up to my front door to grab the package. I turned back around to leave and just froze. My heart was racing and my stomach dropped. Looking back at my new car, all I could think was, "That's not my car! This isn't my life!" I almost couldn't force my legs to get me back down the driveway to get back in the car and leave. Why can't I go back and fix this? I don't want this life, but it's the only life I have.

Monday, March 4th, 2013 at 11:47 am
Hard to believe

I spent some time at home yesterday, both alone and with some friends. At times, I was keeping busy and just going about my business. Other times, I just couldn't believe he was not going to come walking around the corner. Sometimes it is so easy to believe he is in the garage, down the hall, or out running errands. He will be back soon. He isn't gone forever. This did not really happen. It's not that I don't believe it happened. I know it did. It is just so much nicer to think he will come walking in the door at any point.

I have started some plans for moving back home. I know

I can do it. It will not be easy, but I need to begin moving on. Ha! Moving on. I use that term loosely. It will be a long time until I can actually "move on," but I need to take some steps. I think there will be a lot of nights of reminding myself that he is not coming home. God, how I would love to see his face come through the door again!

Tuesday, March 5th, 2013 at 12:06 pm
Reminders

A week or two before Alex's passing, we had gotten into an argument about gun safety. Surprised? He was angrily saying I had clearly not done enough research if I was not on board with getting my own gun and going to gun classes, etc. I was angry because he had gotten to the point of not respecting my opinion whatsoever anymore when it came to shooting games and gun-related activities.

He was always the insulter in arguments. We would even laugh about it later. He would get angry, say some really mean things, and then refuse to talk about it anymore and go about his business or just go to bed like normal. I, on the other hand, want to discuss the crap out of it, resolve it, and move on. If I can't, I stay mad and stew. I will fight until you can prove me wrong and I 100% admit that. If you can prove me wrong then I WILL apologize. It would never get to someone being right or wrong because he would refuse to finish any argument.

On this day, Alex went to bed. The next morning, I left for work early and came home late. I work a lot of 12+ hour days. When I walked in the door, he handed me roses and a note. "*I'm sorry. Love you, Mom.*" He had never done that before. It was very sweet. The card is still on my fridge. I don't know that I'll ever move it. I almost look at it now as if it says he's sorry for dying. I know that's not what it means, but that's how it feels.

Wednesday, March 6th, 2013 at 1:27 pm
Hope

I find hope in the thought that I may someday find happiness again. Right now, the idea seems completely unimaginable. People on the outside of this situation seem to discuss what the right amount of time is before someone can start dating again. As someone on the inside, I can honestly say I have no idea. The thought of dating at this point is revolting. I hope I don't feel that way in twenty years. I want HIM and I can't have him. I fear that no one will ever match up and I will never be able to love someone as much as I love him. It was once said on "Grey's Anatomy" that it would be a pretty messed up system if a person had only one soul mate. If we do only have one soul mate, he was mine, and I lost him. I am so thankful I had six years with him. Some people never get that. He gave me the best gift I could ever ask for, my princess. She is a part of him I will always have. No matter what, he will always have a part of my heart and will always be my husband.

Thursday, March 7th, 2013 at 11:49 pm
Home Sweet Home

This morning, I woke up to NO internet and NO TV. Well, screw that, I'm going home! (Please note the Cartman reference.) Alexa and I spent the day at home and it went rather well. I got a lot done. I went through more of Alexa's clothes, did more organizing, and went through more of Alex's things. I even worked myself up to going in the basement, alone, to get some bins. I even showered in my house! My grandparents came to visit and played with Alexa so I could get even more done. At the end of our time there, I wanted to bring more stuff to the basement, but just did not have the mental energy to do it again. Once was enough. I'm happy I was able to do that.

As, usual I was excited to get the mail, but was only greeted with a $500 ambulance bill from the night Alex died. UGH. Anyway, I dropped Alexa off to my dad and went to therapy. We talked about how I'm memorializing Alex in some ways, yet erasing him in others. That's how it has to be, I guess. My home and my life cannot be a shrine to him. I felt pretty good leaving, as I usually do, until the radio struck again.

"I'm already there. Take a look around. I'm the sunshine in your hair. I'm the shadow on the ground. I'm the whisper in your hair. I'm your imaginary friend."

There was a lot of crying involved in that one.

Saturday, March 9th, 2013 at 3:18 pm
Which Would You Rather?

This has actually come up in discussion more than once as, unfortunately, I know more than one person going through a divorce right now. Would I rather be going through this or going through a divorce? The simple answer is, I don't know. I know that in both situations, your life seems ruined, and there is basically nothing you can do about it.

If I were getting divorced, I would still be losing the person I love, but there are some major differences. I would still have him here and have some answers. Maybe not the answers I want, but answers. My daughter would still have a father. I know that custody and co-parenting can get messy, but she would have two parents that love her. My husband loved me and I love him.

It's hard to be in love with someone dead. I feel that with divorce, moving on to a new relationship is a much quicker option. I worry that I may never get there. Though with breakups, people sometimes move on right away.

Divorce can get messy. Although this is awful and mentally destructive, it's all about moving on. If you have children, you never really move on from their other parent. Financially, either one can destroy you. Divorce may have destroyed me more, who knows. I still would live in a cardboard box to have him back. I do think that although these are very different situations, the emotions involved are similar. There is one huge factor here. I would not have divorced him. By now, we would have had this all figured out and everything could have been okay. At least that's what I want to believe.

Tuesday, March 12th, 2013 at 1:16 am
Sadness

One of the stages of grief is anger. I find myself in that stage a lot. In this situation, it is normal to be angry. But what happens when the anger fades? Anger dulls the sadness and dulls the pain, even if only a little bit.

Tonight, I don't have it in me to be angry at all. I miss him and that's it. I just miss him. I want so bad to see him today. I'm hurting, knowing that I can't. I'm feeling a lot of disbelief today. This afternoon, for a split second, I thought I could text him. Tonight, I had to remind myself I wasn't going home to him. Why does this happen? I don't know. I do know that I cried most of the way home, and will probably still have to reconvince myself that this is real before I can fall asleep.

Wednesday, March 13th, 2013 at 12:29 pm
Triggers

A song ended and the next thing I heard was, "Oh, I just died in your arms tonight." I immediately shut it off, but it was too late. The flashbacks already started. I can't describe my flashbacks without getting graphic, so I won't. My stomach tied in knots. My breathing changed. I started to cry. I tried to rationalize it saying that he really didn't die in my arms and was probably long gone before I got there. You never know where a trigger (for lack of a better term) will be and how you will react. This one caught me off guard!

Thursday, March 14th, 2013 at 10:03 pm
Is Suicide Selfish?

"Suicide is selfish." I've heard a lot of opinions on this and now it's time to form my own.

My initial gut instinct is to say it is selfish. You leave all of your worldly responsibilities to someone else and hurt everyone around you just to ease your pain. But think about this: I am thinking in my right mind. If you are actually to the point of (in this case) pulling the trigger, there is no way you can possibly be thinking clearly enough to understand the selfishness or repercussions of your actions. I'm not talking about thinking about suicide. Anyone can have a weak moment and think the pain can be over if they jump in front of a bus. I mean someone who actually plans, decides, and succeeds. They are obviously not thinking with a sound mind.

Many have commented that Alex thought he was doing a selfless thing. It hurts to think he did this for me, but I believe he did. After reading and re-reading and re-rereading (remember hindsight is 20:20) his texts, he was telling me that his death would be the solution to getting us out of all the debt he caused and all the pain he caused me. Clearly, in his mind, he wasn't able to consider the pain his death would cause me.

I guess my opinion is that it is selfish and yet it isn't. Either way, if that is your opinion, it's not the best thing to say to someone who is grieving the loss of a loved one to suicide. We are already so torn apart with such varying emotions. Comments like that are not productive nor supportive.

Saturday, March 16th, 2013 at 1:24 pm
Firsts…

Tonight will be my first night sleeping in my house. I won't be alone. Well I'll never be alone, since I have so many pets and a child. But for my first night back, I will be having a sleepover! We debated whether it was best to have Alexa there, but decided to let her stay with the grandparents for the night. We're all almost thirty years old now. It's not quite going to be like when we were thirteen, but it'll still be fun. I'm still a little nervous. Wish me luck!

Sunday, March 17th, 2013 at 11:22 pm
Weekend Update

Overall, it was a good weekend. My friends visited. The guest room is set up again and looks pretty good. The living room has been changed a bit, but is not exactly how I want it yet. It's a start. I am moving toward making the house my own. We spent the day hanging home with my little munchkin and the day went fast! At night, it was a girls night out! We have all been friends for so many years, but I don't get to see them often enough.

In between dinner courses at a favorite fondue restaurant, I went outside and thought to myself that I should text Alex to let him know how things were going. Clearly, I forgot. Instead of getting upset, I smiled. I was having so much fun that I forgot the details of my life for a little while.

We stayed out way past my bedtime and headed home for our sleepover. My bed is so comfortable! I don't know if it was having three other girls in my room and two down the hall, the fact that I was so full, that it was 1:30 am, or that I have been sleeping on a futon for so long, but either way, I slept great! I am surprised I slept at all. In the morning, I made breakfast for everyone. I love cooking.

After everyone left, Alexa and I both went for a nap. I really needed it. I'm getting too old to stay out so late! I enjoyed sleeping in my bed again. Later, I made my Sunday trip to the graveyard. I don't know what happened this time, but I got so worked up and hysterical. I was such a mess. I completely fell apart and ended up vomiting. I still feel like crap. On a brighter note, I was happy to see that the base for his headstone has been started. I'm looking forward to that being finished. I'm not sure why. Maybe some closure.

I will be sleeping at my house again tomorrow night. We'll see how that goes. One day at a time.

Tuesday, March 19th, 2013 at 12:48 am
Day Two

Tonight will be the second time sleeping in my house. I went to my parents for dinner after work, packed up, and went home. My dad is staying over to help me get settled. My first reaction coming in was pure anger! I'm mad I have to go through this! I'm mad at him for leaving me alone! I'm mad at all the reminders in the house! Alexa is up past her bedtime. It is her first night here and I don't think she is accepting it well. Every time I think she's asleep, the crying starts again. I may be in for a rough night. We'll see. There are no parenting books on this.

Tuesday, March 19th, 2013 at 9:51 pm
Faux Pas

People use a lot of expressions that don't seem to mean much, until it means something to you. Today, I had a security system installed in my house. I got to talking with the guy since he said he normally works in New Jersey. I mentioned that Alex worked in Howell at one point. He asked if he did the commute from here and when I replied that he did, he said, "If I had to do that commute I would put a bullet in my head." My response? "Well, he did that." I don't believe he had any idea what I meant, but still it makes you think about the things we say.

I have recently encountered "Don't kill yourself," instead of "Don't trip." I've also heard multiple people say "OMG I'm going to kill/shoot myself" over stupid things. Have you heard "I need that like I need a hole in the head?" Yup, caught MYSELF saying that recently. **insert foot in mouth now** Have you ever been frustrated and mimicked shooting yourself in the head? Not kidding, someone did that to me the other day too. Clearly, no one meant any harm by these comments/gestures. Some of them didn't even know the situation. However, it really makes me (try to) think before speaking.

Thursday, March 21ˢᵗ, 2013 at 2:16 am
Counting

Sometimes I feel like I'm just wishing away my life. Every night, I think about how I somehow made it through another day. Every morning, I tell myself I'll somehow get through today too. I count the hours to get through another day. I count the minutes until I'm done being alone with my thoughts in the car. I count the days until I have something, anything, to look forward to. I know that in eleven days, I will have survived three full months of grieving. I hear it gets better after a year. Nine months to go. I've slept in my house three times now. I'm counting those days wondering when it will feel better there. I'm just counting until it stops hurting. Is today over yet?

Saturday, March 23ʳᵈ, 2013 at 2:24 am
I'm All Over The Place

I'm exhausted and a little all over the place tonight. I previously wrote about taking off my rings and wearing them on a chain around my neck. After wearing my "promise ring" for six years, I started to have an allergic reaction to it! It now resides with the rest of my rings on that chain. I like having them there. I am not anywhere near ready to put them away. The issue is, when people ask about them. I am very open about my life and will never lie about any aspect of my life. However, depending on the situation (like at work), I attempt to simply answer the question and move on.

Today, that just couldn't happen. After asking whose rings were around my neck, why they were there, how old my husband was, and how he passed away, a client proceeded to tell me she would shoot herself if she had as many pets as I do. Really?

In the same conversation? It was almost funny. Of course, this same person, when hearing the news, immediately said, "I am so sorry! How awful!"

I am very uncomfortable with the sympathy! I really do appreciate that people care, and always just awkwardly say thank you and try to change the subject. I don't do well with pity and don't want anyone to feel sorry for me. It just makes me feel weird. That being said, I feel the same about myself. I remind myself not to throw a pity party on a regular basis. Sure, I can have bad days, hours, or moments, but I have to pick myself back up. People always tell me I will have good days and bad. Really, I have good moments and bad moments. I can't say that most days are particularly good or bad. They are all both.

I was having a rough moment last night. For the first time in the few nights I have been back home, I had a really hard time with the fact that I was alone in "our bed." I really hated how cold, quiet, and empty it felt without him. I expected to feel that way at some point, but I guess I was so tired each night that I hadn't really let myself think about it. I have really been thrown into living at home.

As I have previously mentioned, I had a security system installed on Tuesday. Since I needed to be home early in the morning, I slept there the night before. When I realized how traumatic it was for Alexa to start sleeping in her room, I decided I could not confuse her anymore, and had to officially stay here every night. She has done better and better each time. It really gave me no option, and thus, I've gone through with it. Nights are still a little strange. As I always say, tomorrow (night) is another day (or in this case, night).

Sunday, March 24th, 2013 at 1:36 am
Saying Hi?

Today was one of those days of constant reminders of him. I met a friend at the mall for a little bit today. For most of the drive there, I was following a silver Honda Civic SI hatchback. This is the car Alex drove when we met and for most of our relationship. I pulled into the parking lot in tears but pulled myself together and went inside.

It wasn't long before I walked past a guy wearing one of Alex's favorite shirts. I brushed it off. Then, we entered the food court. It sounds terrible, but Alex was a little kid at heart and always making jokes. I used to say he was the one that took every joke one step too far. Every time we were at the mall, he would imitate the workers by shouting, "Free sample!" He knew it embarrassed me and always got a kick out of it. When I heard, "Free sample," I immediately thought of him and heard it in his voice. I had to really stifle my laughter. I stepped outside and saw a child run away from his father. The father started yelling, "Alex! Alex! Alex!!" By this point, I had to laugh. I guess he was trying to say hi today!

Tuesday, March 26th, 2013 at 12:15 am
The Good and the Bad

Today felt like an overall crappy day. I rushed out of the house this morning knowing my commute would take exceptionally long because of the snow. I was right. Being stuck in traffic gives me extra anxiety on top of what I already have by being alone with my thoughts.

I thought I had stopped trying to rationalize all this. I

thought I had stopped replaying that night and trying to change what I said. I thought I stopped trying to understand what he was thinking. Apparently, I had just taken a break. In some ways, it had gotten worse. Now, I even picture what exactly happened. I picture him walking down the stairs, texting me, smoking, holding the gun, and so on. I wasn't there to see it, but I try to imagine it. I can't even begin to explain why. The drive gives me the alone time to do this.

I was just in a funk today and just wanted it to be over. I just couldn't focus. The drive home was shorter, but my mind still drove me crazy. Some song played about love conquering all. What crap! By the time I got home, I was exhausted and a mess. I just wanted to be curled up and crying, but I didn't. At the end of the night, Alexa started crawling! I guess she knew I could use a smile. Every day has some good and some bad.

Wednesday, March 27th, 2013 at 11:13 am
The Stages of Grief

I'm sure everyone has heard of the stages of grief. I had previously. But, did you know that it doesn't go in order and you can be in any stage at any time and then switch? I didn't. Depending on which article you are reading, there are different names and sometimes even a different number of stages. My main two are sadness and anger, but I go back to bargaining and denial sometimes too. Depression is always hanging around.

You would think I would be way past denial. I'm not. Sometimes I think denial is my way of getting through each day. If I can block out what's happening, I can function. Last night, sadness and anger really got a hold of me. I sold his workout bench. There is no reason for me to keep it. I thought I was okay with it, until it was actually happening. I guess the thought that it was the last tangible item he touched started to hit me. Watching it go out the door, I got hysterical and made myself sick. I'm really getting sick of that happening. I felt sick the rest of the night and went to bed early. Well, not really early for me, but for the rest of the world. I fell asleep quickly, which usually doesn't happen.

A few hours later, I woke up feeling extremely angry. Not only was I angry that he ruined my life, but angry at everything he had done prior and everything that originally made me angry that day. I was just livid thinking about all the lies, and the lies that were used to cover those original lies.

How could he do that to me? How could I be so blind? I was even more pissed off that he was gone, and I was given no opportunity to fix everything. I have no real explanation for anything. All these lies were dumped on me, and then he was gone.

I don't even know how long I laid there before finally falling back asleep, but it wasn't long before I had a crying baby. She used to sleep through the night, but with all the life changes, she doesn't anymore. She is great and it doesn't take me long to get her back to bed, but it takes a very long time for me to get back to bed.

Morning came too fast, and I'm just tired and depressed. There's no real sadness or anger or anything else really. Just depression. Hopefully writing, showering, and some coffee will get me going. I'm kicking myself for scheduling an eye exam before work. I'd love to cancel and go back to bed, but I really need to order more contacts. I've been wearing these for at least four months. Here I go.

Thursday, March 28th, 2013 at 9:47 pm
Rent

With my birthday quickly approaching, I was thinking

about my past birthdays. For my twenty-fourth birthday, one month before our wedding, Alex and I and another couple we were/are close with went to see "Rent" on Broadway. It was a great day! Today, I listened to the soundtrack. Nothing like suicide, New Year's, betrayal, misery, and death all rolled into a neat little package to start my day! It was amazing to see the different meaning the lyrics took on now.

I will be turning twenty-nine soon, and I just cannot believe how life became so different. I was listening to the soundtrack while driving around with my ten-month-old today. (I forgot about the cursing in it, oops!) Five years ago, I was watching the play with my soon-to-be husband, who is now dead. How did this happen? I couldn't help but think over and over, *"Will I wake from this nightmare."* They were describing my life through song!

"Without you, the ground thaws, the rain falls, the grass grows. Without you, the seeds root, the flowers bloom, the children play, the stars gleam, the poets dream, the eagles fly. Without you, the earth turns, the sun burns..."

"The heart may freeze, or it can burn. The pain will ease, if I can learn. There is no future, there is no past. I live this moment as my last. There's only us. There's only this. Forget regret or life is yours to miss. No other road. No other day. No day but today."

Friday, March 29th, 2013 at 8:42 pm
Am I Seeing Things?

Today started rather well. Alexa and I both slept through

the night. I had a bit of a headache, but that is nothing new for me. Of course, I made my usual stop at Dunkin Donuts and had my normal dose of caffeine with my multigrain bagel. Traffic was not bad at all! I got to work early and my headache started to subside. We were busy and I just kept going. My mind had no chance to wander. Then, lunchtime came.

I took my usual walk and was headed back into work. Suddenly, I swore I was seeing things. From a distance, I could see the bright blue color of Alex's car. I should not be surprised, as someone that works here bought the car for a family member. I started to walk toward it, then changed my mind. I was sure it was his, but what was the point of getting close? I never really thought I would see it. It felt so very strange! But at the same time, not so strange. I did not get upset. My whole life is a reminder. Why should this be any different?

Saturday, March 30th, 2013 at 12:26 pm
My Life

Since starting this blog, I have been in contact with many people I probably wouldn't have otherwise. Some are friends and acquaintances I lost contact with long ago, and others are people I have never even met. Opening up my life to the world has made people comfortable with opening up to me. I like this. For one thing, it makes me feel a little less alone in my situation when people can relate, even in just a tiny way. Second, I can't put into words what it means to me that my stories are helping people cope, understand, and have hope.

Something that has come up on multiple occasions (and I just can't believe how common this is) is readers who have loved ones who have attempted and failed at completing suicide or have threatened/had suicidal thoughts. Here is my best advice. I believe that people that are in that frame of mind are not thinking of the aftermath. They are in that moment and ultimately thinking of a permanent solution to a temporary problem. They can't see how it affects those around them. Only that the pain (whatever it is) will be over for them.

My answer is, show them this. Let them into my life. I AM the aftermath. My world is a product of suicide. My daughter, one day, will understand her place in the aftermath of suicide. I am certain that if Alex could have comprehended what my life would be like now, he may have chosen a different path. If I can save a life or help a relationship, he wouldn't have died in vain and my pain will be worth something. I don't want others to hurt like I do.

Sunday, March 31st, 2013 at 10:49 am
Easter

Well here I am again, writing that a holiday is "just another day." Alexa isn't old enough to understand, so it's not like I really have to do anything to celebrate her first Easter. I had her picture taken with the Easter bunny recently at least. I didn't have it in me (or the time) to make Easter bread or dye eggs this year. The bread is so time-consuming and Alex ate most of it anyway. I indulged in a few Cadbury cream eggs over the past few weeks though. I am working today too. Someone has to and I don't mind.

Today is also three months since Alex's death. I made it this far. Part of me feels like it just happened yesterday, and another part feels like I've been without him for so long. I don't think that will change for a while. It may be the three month anniversary, but today doesn't really feel any different than any other day, I think.

April 2013

Tuesday, April 2nd, 2013 at 2:01 am
I Wish...

I often find that there are many times when I think, "I wish I could ask Alex" or "Wish he were around to tell him that." I got a message today asking advice on a camera purchase. I can tell you all about my cameras. You want to know everything there is to know about every camera and lens available? You would have to ask Alex.

Tomorrow, I am headed to a bird store/breeder for work and fun. It is near where Alex worked. How do I get there? He would know! Boy, I wish I could remember what he told me about finding the place when we discussed it months ago.

My internet keeps cutting out. My computer tells me, "Contact your IT administrator." Umm, I don't have one anymore. Any computer issues used to mean, "Mow, help?"

I am on the email list for thinkgeek.com because he loved stuff from that site. I always find things I wish I could show him or buy for him. There are always stupid questions like "Why do you have one bicycle rim in the basement and one in the garage?" While cleaning, I found a trophy one of us won on our honeymoon. I can't remember who won it or how. I wonder if he would.

A friend of mine is on a dating site. She sent me a screenshot of a bunch of people who messaged her. I recognized one as a guy Alex and I knew years ago. It drove me crazy trying to remember his name. I was sure Alex would know. I did remember eventually.

There are items of his I would really like to know what he would like me to do with them now. I wish he could just tell me.

Going through his ridiculous amounts of tools brought up questions. I'm not kidding, twenty pairs of pliers. At least I could identify those. What are some of these things? Where did they come from? I was always under the impression that his tools belonged to work. They don't. More things he was buying behind my back? It's a rather impressive collection. I guess it would be if I knew anything about tools. I thought I knew enough about bike parts. Some of these things I can't even identify. I'd love to ask what they are, what they are worth, and what I should do with them. He wanted Alexa to learn to solve a Rubik's Cube. How do I learn to teach her? The list goes on and on.

Wednesday, April 3rd, 2013 at 4:19 pm
Nothing?

I was really sick yesterday. My sinus infection came back with a vengeance. I didn't have the energy to do much of anything and I'm still sick today, but at least functioning.

I've read about widows having days of feeling "nothing," but it hadn't happened to me yet. Yesterday, it did. Maybe because I felt like crap and just couldn't think of anything else, I don't know. I looked at his photo and literally felt nothing. There was no love, anger, or sadness. It reminded me of the lyrics, *"Now you're just somebody that I used to know."* Of course, that didn't last long, and today, I'm right back where I was. Looking at the same photo today, I miss him. No surprises there.

Monday, April 8th, 2013 at 1:27 am
It's My Party and I'll Cry if I Want to

But I didn't...

A few months ago, a friend and I planned a joint birthday party. It seemed like a good idea at the time. I felt that it was a long way off, and I would be ready to celebrate by then. I was really looking forward to it. I had been counting down for a while. A few days ago, I got sick again. AGAIN!! My cough is just out of control. I've been feeling lousy for a week. All I could think about was getting better for my birthday party.

I (obviously) have been very down on myself and not looking very good lately. I had debated a haircut and even thought about maybe going to get some hair dye. Friday morning, I was just hanging around feeling crappy, mentally and physically, when my mom called. She thought it would be a good idea to get out and get my hair done.

For my birthday present, I became a redhead again. I pulled up a photo from my twenty-fifth birthday and said, "I want this!" The hairdresser asked why and I told her I was trying to get in the spirit for my twenty-ninth birthday because I was not very excited. She said, "But twenty-nine is a great year!" I replied, "Well, no, my husband just died." What else could I say?

That took all my energy and I went home and took a very long nap. I woke up Saturday morning not feeling very good, but well enough to go. Thankfully, one of my best friends had already driven down from Massachusetts the night before, so I would not have to be alone in the car all the way to New Jersey. You all know how I feel about being alone with my thoughts. I had been worrying over the past few weeks about the fact that this was a joint party, and there may be people I didn't know. I am much more comfortable around my close friends. With large groups of people, I don't know who knows about my life and how much they know. Therefore, I am always worried about how I act and what I say. It sounds stupid, but it is the root of my social anxiety now. I know at some point, I have to let this go.

We drove up to the hotel, got ready, and the anxiety began. I suddenly did not want to go. I knew it was too late to call the whole thing off, but I wanted to. Why did I agree to this? I did NOT want to celebrate my birthday without him. I was dressed up, wearing makeup and heels, and had brand new red hair. Who am I? I didn't even recognize myself and wanted to just take it all off and curl up in bed. Of course, I didn't and forced myself back in the car and headed to the party. As usual, that was the hardest part.

I took a deep breath, and went inside. I saw my friends, had a good time, talked about good memories of Alex (and some of the bad stuff). After dinner, we went bowling. Man, am I terrible at bowling, but it was still fun. A friend mistakenly referred to me as "Heather and Alex." I'm sure she felt bad, but I didn't. It was habit. We were Heather and Alex, and in a way, we still are. He is always a part of me.

We didn't get back to the hotel until 1am, way past my bedtime, but this was probably the first time I did not have a baby to get up with. I usually wake up very early, even when I go to bed late, but I woke up at 9:40! I couldn't believe it. We met some friends for lunch and grabbed some NJ lottery tickets and bagels. We made a stop at the Filipino grocery store (we don't have one here) for a few things I like, and then headed back to Delaware.

Along the way, we passed places with a lot of memories associated with them. The place we met, restaurants we went to, roads we took, and so on. Sometimes, it felt strange. Other times, I hardly noticed. I am never going to escape reminders, and that's okay. We got back home and picked up Alexa. I missed her. I'm not sure I realized it until I saw her.

My life was so different this weekend that I didn't notice how weird it was not to have her with me. When I got home, I got to see the cherry blossom tree my dad planted in my front yard. Alex always talked about getting a cherry blossom tattoo, but never did, so this is for him. It doesn't look like much now, but one day, it will. I didn't get through my first birthday without him yet, but I got through my first birthday party without him. Thank you so much to everyone who was a part of it.

Monday, April 8th, 2013 at 11:22 pm
A Few Quick Thoughts

It was just a few days ago when I was said I saw Alex's old car at work. Although it seemed strange, it didn't really bother me either. Today was a different story. It was in the parking lot when I left. I was just talking to the current driver about how it was no big deal. For some reason, after getting in my truck and getting ready to drive off, it became a big deal. I burst into tears and had to wait a few minutes to calm down and work myself up to drive past it to be able to get out of the parking lot. It's interesting how some days the same thing will bother you that doesn't on other days.

It's been awhile since I complained about insurance, but here I go again. I recently got a bill in the mail for $500 for MY ambulance ride to the hospital for my blood pressure the night he died. Mind you, the EMS was already at my house for him, but took me instead. Well the $500 went to my deductible so fine, whatever, I paid it. Now, I get another bill in the mail for $475. This bill is his. Why do I owe this? Insurance denied it saying his insurance ended that day. Why did his insurance end that day? Because he died! Why did I call an ambulance? Because he died! You just can't make this stuff up!

Thursday, April 11th, 2013 at 2:02 am
Widow/Single Mom

Through the power that is Google Analytics, I can see what people have searched that brought up my page. One that struck me as interesting was "I am not a single mom, I'm a widow." Well the two aren't mutually exclusive, are they? I AM a widow and I AM a single mom. I think I see what they are getting at, though. As a widow, it is tough to fit in with other single moms, as their situations are typically pretty different. I have attempted to join some single mom groups online and it is not a good fit for me. Posts usually revolve around discussing issues with the ex, weekends without children, etc. I can't relate to any of that. I don't feel like I fit in well in widow groups either. There aren't too many twenty-eight-year-old widows out there. Where do I fit in?

Thursday, April 11th, 2013 at 8:10 pm
The Big Day

Today was a big day I guess, one hundred days since his death. I didn't even realize, as I haven't been counting, until my mom mentioned it today. Wow, one hundred days. Today was also a big day I've been waiting for, the day the stone arrived. One of Alex's closest friends drove down to see it with me. It is beautiful! I cried when I saw it, which I expected, but I am truly amazed at how perfect it is.

I'm glad this part is over. The anxiety has been building all week and I just couldn't keep my mind off it. Something that had been bothering me lately is the phrase "headstone." Typically, the stone is placed at the head of the person. In this case, it is at his feet. Because of the manner in which Alex passed away and the fact that I wanted an open casket for the funeral, things were done a little differently. When going to a wake, the person's head is usually to the left side of the room. His was to the right. I was told that the casket is lowered into the ground exactly as you see it at the graveside ceremony. Therefore, he is backward and the stone is at his feet. Seemed weird at first, but now it's funny.

Leave it to Alex to be buried backwards! Sounds about right.

Saturday, April 12th, 2013 at 11:59 pm
I'm 29

Today started with of the most depressing moments I've had. I knew it would be hard, but did not expect to feel so awful. I did not want to get out of bed, and when I finally did, I just felt like I had to sit down and couldn't move. It was pouring outside, mimicking my mood. I felt like I could just sit in the garage watching the rain all day. My mom came over to help me out, and I decided to run out in the crazy rain for McDonald's breakfast. Breakfast and coffee helped for a bit.

I was dreading the fact that I had to go to work in a few hours. I really just wanted the day to be over already. I would have rather skipped it completely, and never even acknowledged that it was my birthday. Clearly, that was not going to happen.

I felt better getting to work, as it was a rather normal day. I didn't have to think much about what today was. All I can really say is, I did it. The day is almost over. I made it through and tomorrow will be back to normal. Someone even asked me if I was turning twenty-one today! I'm not sure how I feel about that.

I very much appreciate everyone's well wishes today. Although I hate to say it, "Happy Birthday" does not seem like quite the appropriate feeling this year. I am not sure next year will be much better. I'll still be a widow and instead of turning twenty-nine, I'll be turning thirty. At least the plaque for Alex's memorial tree came in today. Just like the gravestone, it is beautiful. I look forward to putting it in my yard.

Tuesday, April 16th, 2013 at 1:33 am
Terms and Titles

This seems to be tripping me up a lot lately. What am I supposed to refer to Alex as? Calling him my husband infers that I am currently married and he is around. Going by ex-husband is not accurate. We aren't divorced, but technically he's no longer my husband, right? I thought a lot about "former husband," but that doesn't really sound right either. I know that the proper term is "late husband," but why do we say that? He's not running late. He's not coming back. It's obviously not appropriate to say "my dead husband," but that is the most accurate! I think there needs to be a better term for this. I've also wondered if I still go by Mrs. or am I Miss again? The easy answer is to go by Ms. but that wasn't a good enough answer for me, of course. After looking into it, the answer is a widow is still considered Mrs. In the scheme of things, none of this should really matter, but these are the random things I think about.

Tuesday, April 16th, 2013 at 10:04 pm
Not What I Expected

I had a totally different blog topic picked for today. However, today has not been at all what I expected and has changed the direction of this post a bit. (Maybe I'll fit in another one later.)

First, I was able to finally get Alex's phone back from the police and was given some interesting information. During the investigation, the detective contacted his employer. He was told that Alex was amazing and they loved him (blah blah blah), but also that he was continually borrowing money from them. Well that was news to me! I must admit, that angered me.

I went down to the graveyard to leave some flowers, but really did not feel like being there. I was happy to see little bits of grass starting to grow though. The first thing I noticed on his phone was the fact that a good portion of apps were deleted. I immediately went to his texts, and many of those seemed to be missing as well.

The only information I was really able to get was he told a co-worker that day that he "needed a way out of this mess," and the last text he sent was telling the same co-worker to give someone a gun. Not really sure what that meant. Looking through the timestamps on his phone, seeing my twelve missed calls, and the deleted apps made me feel like I was reliving the night he died.

I feel awful, angry, and sad. I can't help but be angry that he knew what he was doing. He specifically deleted emails, texts, apps, etc. Why? What did it matter anymore?

It was not the end of the day as I still had to go grocery shopping. I tried to calm myself down but just had so much anxiety. Plus, Alexa will not stop saying dada today. Everywhere we went all day long, all through the store, "Dada dada dada dada." I just wanted to scream at her to stop, but I knew I couldn't. It's not her fault I'm upset. UGH!

Friday, April 19th, 2013 at 2:49 am
No Escape

Sometimes I just want to escape my life for a little while. I don't want the anger and pain in the back of my mind all the time. I want to have a day where I'm not reminded of him and the fact that he's gone. I want one day where I don't hear an upsetting song. I want a day where the gun references don't bother me. I want to stop worrying about what else I'm going to find out.

When will I be done putting together the pieces and analyzing everything?

I'd like to just be a mom, not a single mom. I'd like to not be defined by this one terrible experience. But how can you not be? Can I have a day where every responsibility is taken care of so I can just breathe and grieve? When will I stop loving someone who is gone? I'd like a day without that pain. When will I stop thinking of every point in time as before he died vs. after he died? Do I ever get to just be me again? Have you ever gotten sick of dealing with something? Well tonight I'm there. I want my life back!

Tuesday, April 23rd, 2013 at 5:43 pm
Eleven Months Old

My baby girl is eleven months old today and she's sick again. I've done my best to cover my work hours to stay home with her for the next few days. Nothing like paying for daycare that she can't go to. Sometimes it's a lot to deal with, but I would do anything for her. That's my job as a mom and I'm happy to do it.

However, I can't help but get angry that Alex didn't hold up his end of the parent agreement. I'm not supposed to be doing this without him. When you have a child, it is your job to put them before everything else in the world, and I can't help but feel that he didn't. With the anger comes guilt and sadness. I feel awful that I feel this way. He's a good man who made a mistake, but I am paying for that mistake. I wish she had her daddy to hug her right now.

May 2013

Wednesday, May 1st, 2013 at 1:12 am
A Fun Day

Alexa and I had a fun day together. We went for a nice walk when the rain stopped and did some shopping. She even took a long nap so I could catch up on some sleep too! Looking at her today brought on a lot of thinking.

I would do anything to protect her. I feel that my whole purpose in life is to do just that. Right now, she is an innocent, happy baby that only knows the joys of the people around her, her love for our pets, and her excitement for learning new things. I worry that someday I may protect her too much.

I do my best right now to let her learn what she needs to. I let her explore when it's safe and try to stand and walk on her own. She has to learn these things. As my only child, will I be too overbearing when she gets older? I hope not. I hate the thought that someday she will grow up and ask where daddy is. I worry about when she's older and I have to explain the truth. Where do I even begin explaining? How will that make her feel? How will that affect her view of her childhood and the type of woman she grows up to be? All I can do for now is look at that beautiful smile, hug my princess, and hope for the best.

Friday, May 3rd, 2013 at 2:13 am
Others Around You

At one point in their life, everyone is given the advice that no matter how bad things seem, someone always has it worse. For a while, I kept thinking that basically everyone I knew could look at me and just be thankful they weren't living my life. I honestly felt that I couldn't think of anyone living a worse nightmare than I was when this all happened.

As time has gone on, I still think I have a pretty terrible story of the damage in my life, but you know what? I have a lot to be thankful for. There are a lot of people out there that do have it worse. Just because I don't know them personally, doesn't mean they don't exist.

We are also taught not to judge people we meet because we have no idea what they may be going through. I have never realized how true this is. To the people that stared at me crying in Toys R Us, you didn't know, but I was picking out an outfit for my seven-month-old to wear to her father's funeral. When I went to Walmart late at night in pajamas and slippers, my husband died a few weeks earlier. My parents and baby were sick and I was taking care of them.

Think about it. That man in the grocery store may have just found out he has cancer. That woman standing outside the maternity store in the mall may have just had (another) miscarriage.

My last tangent for the night ties the two together. Although my life is open to the public via this blog, I don't walk around announcing it to everyone I meet. I'm sure I notice it more now but in dealing with the public, I feel that I've heard a lot of "Well I'm a single mom" or "It's hard because I'm alone." I heard a whole breakup story of a stranger the other day.

All of these are in the form of excuses for one thing or another. Part of me wants to say, "I understand" and the other part strongly fights the urge to say, "Really? Do you want to hear my life?" Clearly, I stick with the first one. While complaining about life to strangers, you have no idea what they could also be going through.

Sunday, May 5th, 2013 at 6:59 pm
Only the Good Die Young

There was a discussion on a widow site recently about taking comfort in the fact that whatever purpose our loved ones had, it must have been fulfilled if their lives have ended. I'm really torn on this. Normally I would agree, however what about when their life ended by suicide? This is clearly one of those things that will be filed under "questions I have that will never be answered."

Would he not have been able to take his life if his purpose was not fulfilled? He had attempted and failed previously long before we met (at least he told me he did). Did he fail because he had something to finish, or did he just do it right this time? What happens if he didn't complete his life mission? Does he have to try again?

I'm still not sure how I feel about reincarnation. I'd say if I had to choose now, I don't believe in it. Just because I don't believe it, doesn't mean I'm right. If he did fulfill his purpose, what was it? He gave me Alexa and a means of helping people. Was that it? Of course, this all rides on the idea that we do each have specific purposes in life. I'd like to believe that either way. Only the good die young.

Thursday, May 9th, 2013 at 8:55 pm
Notes

Sometimes as I go through a day at work, I write notes about my feelings on little pieces of scrap paper. I fold them and put them in my pockets. They get my feelings out, keep my sanity, and get thrown out later. Other times, they actually become my blog post for the day.

Last night, I was way too tired and sick to look at them and make sense of it all. I got home and went straight to bed. Today, I decided I'm going to post my notes as-is to show my mindset throughout the day yesterday. I'm happy to say that I'm mentally in a bit of a better place today.

1. I've been hanging out in this "numb" stage. I like it there. Nothing really bothers me too much and I can live my life. I actually thought I had made it to "acceptance." NOPE! Today I'm angry, sad, lonely, and just plain bitter. Here we go again.

2. I'm sick of my life. I want my old life back. This is not the life I wanted for myself or my daughter. There's nothing I can do about it but "just keep swimming."

3. I got to snuggle with a 1.5 pound puppy today. I really needed that. Nothing like puppy therapy. Well maybe Alexa therapy.

4. What's that song I keep hearing about being bent and not broken?

5. I'm pretty sure at this point I'm broken.

6. Tonight, I want to dive into a bowl of frosted flakes or a vat of chocolate ice cream. I want to eat a large Wawa sub or down some mudslides, but I promised myself I wouldn't. I'll be angry at myself if I do.

7. Listening to Adele's voice is making me want to kick the radio.

8. I want to cry so bad. I'm sitting here holding back the tears. I could use a good cry to get it all out. What I can't use is the vomiting and headache that usually follows. Ugh.

9. No matter what, I'll never regret marrying him.

Sunday, May 12th, 2013 at 12:58 am
Step One

People tell me all the time that I am so strong and doing so well. Days like today make me wonder if I'm really not and I'm just great at faking it. I've never cried so many times in one day in my life and it's not even 9 pm. I don't even think I cried this much at the funeral. I just can't hold it together today and honestly, I don't know why.

I don't know what makes today different than any other day in these last few months. I know it is normal to have hard times after doing well for some time, but I feel like I'm starting over from step one. Tonight's pain is almost unbearable and there is absolutely nothing I can do about it.

I ate like crap today and I really don't care. I kept thinking about wanting to come home to some sort of surprise. Ultimately the only surprise I want is for this to have all been a dream and for him to be greeting me at the door. All I can really say is I am so thankful for being able to come home to my little girl. I could not do this without her and I am amazed that during what feels like one of the lowest days of my life, she can still get a smile out of me.

Tomorrow is my first Mother's Day. I should be looking forward to it, and although I hate to say it, I'm dreading it. I'm going to try to make the best of it. I need to stop crying long enough to get rid of this headache if I'm even going to attempt to do anything enjoyable tomorrow.

Sunday, May 19th, 2013 at 10:47 pm
What a Weekend!

It was time to celebrate Alexa's first birthday! I'm learning that the days leading up to an event are the hardest. The day before Mother's Day was horrible. I cried all day, and then the actual holiday was fine.

This week, I spent a lot of time picturing myself faking a smile and pretending to be happy. I worried about breaking down in the middle of the party and crying in front of everyone. I felt that I may not be able to fully enjoy my daughter turning one without Alex. On top of the party, I was having a yard sale that morning, just to stretch my sanity a little further. It was the development yard sale and I did not want to miss that opportunity. I knew it may be rough to watch some of Alex's items leave and some of Alexa's baby stuff sell. Why not add more to an emotional day?

I had everything out in the driveway by 7 am and things were selling right away. Taking Alex's clothes out of the bin to sell did not bother me as much as I thought. Even washed, they still had that Alex smell. I still wear so many of his other clothes. Maybe that's why. My mom asked if she should do that for me, but ultimately, it doesn't matter. Nothing will bring him back and I have to get used to that. I think maybe I am starting to get used to that. Today, anyway. As far as sales, I did well. I sold enough to pay for Alexa's party. Not bad for just grabbing whatever I could in one day. Fifteen minutes before the party was supposed to start, I packed everything up, cleaned myself up, dressed Alexa, and was ready! The party started right away!

Alexa looked like a perfect princess. Her cake was perfect and she smashed it just like I wanted her to. I was surrounded by people I care about and had a good time. I wish Alex could have been there, but I did not let it ruin this day. It is an important milestone in Alexa's life and mine. I am so thankful for such amazing friends and family. I was so stressed out and anxious for everything leading up to the day, but the day was great. It was the best day I have had since Alex died!

Wednesday, May 21st, 2013 at 2:13 am
One Year..

This week last year was, until that point, probably the scariest week of my life. I'm not sure I even realized it at the time. I was pregnant and due on July 12th. I thought I still had a long way to go. It was Friday and the day before my baby shower. Some of my friends had already arrived. I had already been put on modified bed rest and my doctors were concerned about things that had been an issue throughout my entire pregnancy, but this weekend was about me, and I was excited!

A friend and I were in the Dunkin Donuts drive-thru (surprised?) when my phone rang. It was my doctor telling me my lab results came in and I was to immediately head to the hospital. My first response was, "But my baby shower is tomorrow!" Obviously that didn't change her mind. All I could think was I still had eight weeks to go. I had to stay in the hospital for two months?! It was at that point that I realized I could be having Alexa in the next few days. As stubborn as I am, I decided I didn't care and I would go to the hospital AFTER the party. Somehow, hours later, Alex and I were walking into Labor and Delivery and the party was getting cancelled.

A few days passed and I started getting comfortable with my daily 6 am visits from the doctor, constant blood pressure checks, daily ultrasounds, measuring my pee (fun stuff), eating hospital food, and begging to shower. Little did I know that two days from today, my life would change forever.

Friday, May 23rd, 2013 at 12:46 am
Happy Birthday, Alexa!

One year ago today:

As usual, I was stuck laying in my hospital bed. I had just finished my lunch when the on-call OB and my high-risk doctor walked into the room together. Oh no, this can't be good. I was told that today was the day. When I said, "Today?" the response was, "Do you have anything better to do today?" Well, I guess not. Anyway, we could not wait any longer.

I asked if I could be induced and have her naturally, but I was told we cannot wait that long. She has to come out NOW. I called Alex to come quick. Before I knew it, a wheelchair arrived and I was taken to pre-op. Before long, I was prepped and rolled into the surgery suite. It seemed like Alexa was out in only minutes. She did not cry, but made two small little sounds.

The NICU nurses were waiting. They cleaned her up, told me to kiss her, and ran. They were able to tell me that she weighed three pounds, seven ounces and she was breathing. She stopped breathing shortly after and had to be intubated. Not only did she stop breathing, but so did I. I don't know much after that. All the stress was on Alex because after that point, I was fully under anesthesia. I was not aware of anything until the next afternoon. Alexa spent twenty-three days in the NICU and I am so grateful for the care they gave her. It was a rough experience but every moment was worth it!

Today:

This morning, I woke up in the bad place. What I mean by that is, the depression and feeling of loss was overwhelming. If it weren't for the screaming baby, I could have just laid in bed all day sulking and crying.

I knew this was not fair to her. I also knew I needed to get out of this house. I met up with a friend and we went out and celebrated. Alexa got her first Build-a-Bear, wore her birthday dress again, went out to lunch, and visited the animals at work! We had a great time today! Overall, I think it was a great way to spend her first birthday.

Tonight, I said to Alexa, "Well, Mommy made it through a year." Then I followed it with, "Sure wish daddy did." I started the day with tears and ended the day with tears, but the middle was very good.

Saturday, May 25th, 2013 at 2:15 am
Moving Forward

Some nights, I want nothing more than to know I'm going home to him. I can almost convince myself that I am. Almost. This morning was one of those mornings where all I could do is scream at him until I cried. I'm not sure if he can hear my thoughts, but I'm fairly certain he can hear what I'm saying.

I'm still angry tonight, but anger or not, I wish I could come home to a "mow" hug. Either way, I feel I've made some progress. Recently, in the middle of the night when I couldn't sleep, I got the courage to change my Facebook relationship status to widowed. I know it's just Facebook, but that was a big step for me. I guess at that moment, I was ready. I don't always feel like I'm moving forward, but I guess I am.

Sunday, May 26th, 2013 at 10:51 pm
Yeah… That's Probably Weird

This morning, I got up with the goal of cleaning my room. I constantly wash clothes and never put them away. After cleaning, I started going through the clothes that end up in the bottom of my closet and found the bag of clothes from that night. Clearly, they are destroyed. I took them out of the bag. They were still in a crumpled mess and half inside out. I straightened them out, looked them over, folded them nicely, and put them back. I'm not sure why I feel the need to keep them, but I do, and I guess that's all that matters. Still, that's probably weird.

I know this may be a hard week. Five years ago, this was the week leading up to our wedding. I'm trying to focus on the happy memories, but that may be impossible. On the actual day, I will be working for twelve hours. A good distraction, maybe. Like everything else, I will get through it, somehow.

Tuesday, May 28th, 2013 at 1:51 pm
My World

When do the random meltdowns end? While driving home last night, I am not even sure what I was thinking about, but I got myself so worked up that I was completely hysterical by the time I walked in the door. I was hurting knowing (again) that he wouldn't be there when I got home. You would think after almost five months, I would be used to this by now. I guess sometimes I'm not.

Nights are lonely. I miss my kiss goodnight. I want to hold someone's hand again. My bed is big, cold, and empty. I miss laying on his chest, listening to his heartbeat. I miss having a guy to smell and a big teddy bear to hug. I miss being in love. I miss having someone to be silly and giggle with. I miss intimacy. I miss being so very comfortable with another person.

Watching people text with their significant others has gotten hard too. I miss that. I talked to a friend about it who felt that it was a good thing. It's a big step for me to admit that I'm lonely and want that again someday. I get lonely and the anger starts again. How did he not know that I love him enough to get through this? How could he think this was better for me? No matter what, I did not want to lose him. I doesn't matter how angry I was and am. I took vows and wouldn't go back on them.

With our anniversary coming up, I think about those vows more. I can't help but feel he didn't honor them. How could you do this to your wife? How could you do this to everyone else in your life that loved you so much? You left behind a family and friends that you meant the world to. Did you not know what you meant to us? I was very angry at what you did. I would like to believe I have forgiven you, knowing you were sick and couldn't help it. Forgive and forget are two different things though.

Last night while lying in bed, I continued reading a book I had been enjoying. I find myself escaping into someone else's world. Late in the book came descriptions of gunshot wounds to the head and attempted suicide. This was not much of an escape anymore and too much like my life.

Reminders are everywhere. I did not sleep well last night and am sore from yesterday's workout. Thankfully I'm off today and pretty much just plan to hang out with Alexa. Sometimes just that is a workout! It's rainy and miserable out. That never helps my mood. Hoping my Keurig and one-year-old can cheer me up!

Tuesday, May 28th, 2013 at 8:43 pm
Poop!

I know what you must be thinking. "She's writing about poop?!" I am, but really, it's about my state of mind. I was at my chiropractor appointment, which also happens to be where my mom works. I was waiting for my turn when I noticed that familiar smell. Uh oh, another dirty diaper. I began to change Alexa and man, was it bad. I had to change her clothes as well. I called mom for backup. As I slid the diaper out from under her, the large pile of feces went flying out of the diaper toward mom. *Splat* It hit the floor. Alexa was up on the table, waiting to finish being changed and I was laughing so hard I was on the floor. I cannot remember the last time I laughed so hard. I had tears in my eyes, and finally in a good way. I pictured Alex there laughing at us, which made me crack up more. He would have loved seeing that! Yup, it took poop to get a good laugh out of me, but man it felt good!

Thursday, May 30th, 2013 at 2:24 pm
The Day Before...

So here it is, the day before another big day. Tomorrow is the five year anniversary of one of the best days of my life, our wedding day. Five years ago today, we were getting everything together, checking into the hotel, and going to our rehearsal dinner. Not before I sat at my kitchen table, broke the chair, and landed on my ass, though. At least I have that to laugh about. It was a wonderful day with friends and family. Before we knew it, it was over and we had one day to relax before leaving for our honeymoon.

Today is so different. It's a regular day. I'm home for the moment and have a lot of errands to run. Since I have to work tomorrow, I will be bringing Alex's anniversary gifts to the graveyard today. It seems strange because there's really nothing to celebrate anymore. He's gone. We aren't married anymore. Maybe it would be easier not to acknowledge the day whatsoever. I guess I felt that way about my birthday too. May is really kicking my ass. Either way, I will never regret our wedding day.

June 2013

Sunday, June 2nd, 2013 at 3:44 am
Single

All in various situations, my single friends are dating, or at least looking to date. I, on the other hand, am single, but basically in a holding pattern. I want to want to date. Does that make sense? I want to be ready, but know I'm not. I have this vision of falling in love and the pain being gone. I know that isn't really how it works.

On the other hand, I have no desire to be involved in the dating world. I'm not much of a catch like this anyway. I don't think I will ever stop loving Alex. I guess, in some way, that love needs to change if I am ever to move on. I don't know how that works. I have to believe he would want me to be happy and not be alone. Still, I want him and no one will ever be him. None of this makes sense, even in my own head. I wasn't supposed to ever be lonely. We were supposed to be together forever. I want to be a family again.

Thursday, June 6th, 2013 at 12:33 pm
Happy?

Recently, while texting with a friend, she commented that someday I will be happy again. Interestingly enough, my gut instinct was to reply, "Well I am happy." I thought about it for a second, suddenly felt horribly guilty, and could not hit send. Days passed and as usual, a Kelly Clarkson song brought this up again,

"My life would suck without you." Again, I thought, "Well my whole life doesn't suck." And again, guilt got me and I felt awful for thinking that.

The more I've pondered it, the more I realize my life doesn't always suck. I am happy sometimes. One large aspect of my life sucks. Otherwise, I have a lot to be thankful for. I'm not going to feel guilty that, when it comes down to it, being a mom is giving me a happy life right now. That does not mean I do not get hystcrical to the point of practically hyperventilating just because I miss him. Last night, I did.

Sunday, June 9th, 2013 at 3:14 am
Family Day

In the time I was with Alex, he was never very close with his family, geographically or emotionally. Therefore, neither was I. I did not know them very well and had not spent much time with them. Life was busy and travel was hard. I'm not really sure what his hesitation was to have a real relationship with them and I guess now I never will. What I do know is I did not feel it was my place to get involved and let him handle it. I guess I always had some awkwardness/resentment through him.

When he passed away and everyone was here for the funeral, I was in such shock. I feel like I can barely remember my interactions with anyone. Things were also overshadowed by everyone meeting Alexa. I've maintained intermittent contact via text and kept things mainly about Alexa.

Yesterday, after five months, was the first subsequent visit. I was nervous, to say the least. I'm a different person now. I did not know what to expect. I had never been alone with them. Saying "them" seems rude but I don't mean any disrespect. I mean only that, this was HIS family. They don't know me well.

This could be an emotional interaction and I had to do it alone. Ultimately, I was not alone, as my grandfather was with me. It was a very rainy day and I needed someone to stay in the car when we were at the graveyard. I am so thankful I had his help and that he thought of it! It was a little tough on Alexa, but she did okay. She is too young to understand who I am handing her over to, and is teething as well. (She got tooth number four today!) She apparently did better when I was not in the room to cling onto.

Watching his family stand at his grave was hard and I could not help but cry. After five months, it was finally time to talk them through that day and explain everything that surrounded it. I promised not to lie, but I did not want to hurt them. It hurt to watch them cry and turn away. I couldn't help but keep saying what a good man he was and how much I love him. It's the truth and that's how I want him to be remembered. I don't want them to think badly of their son. I don't think badly of him. I felt bad hearing how much they were hurting too.

We got through all that and had another birthday celebration for Alexa. It was a happy time for everyone. After they headed back home and I headed to work, his mom told me that I am a great mom and she is sorry for what he did. She also told me I am handling this very well, I picked a great stone, and she knows my family and I loved him very much. This really meant a lot to me. It is unfortunate that I have a relationship with them now, after he is already gone. He meant a lot to all of us. Now we have to all go on without him. With each day brings new challenges, but he is watching me and cheering me on. I wish I could be talking to him tonight.

Wednesday, June 12th, 2013 at 12:39 am
Closure

I got some more closure today. I have the gun back. After over five months, the police finally released it to my dad. I was happy to hear that the detective told my dad, "Alex was a good man. Something just went wrong." This explains it so well. Part of me was dreading opening the envelope. Part of me couldn't wait. I have said before that I am neither for or against guns. I am not afraid of them, but don't really like them either. Not to mention, this is the gun that killed my husband. Ultimately the gun was just the tool, but you know what I mean.

It didn't look anything like I remembered. I didn't even remember it being a revolver. I only saw it really quickly laying there that night, and clearly that was not what I was paying attention to. Holding it in my hand, the dried blood started to flake off. Maybe all of this should have upset me, but it didn't. It felt like a part of him was with me. It felt like I got some closure now.

Sunday, June 16th, 2013 at 12:34 pm
Father's Day

I can't help but feel like this could be a morning of celebrating Alex's second Father's Day, but it isn't and I have to accept that. I am thankful that Alexa is still not old enough to understand what today is. I fear having to explain this to her in future years. How do I explain that everyone is celebrating their dads today, but she doesn't have one? Like everything, I'll figure it all out as time goes on. I want to wish my dad and grandfather a very Happy Father's Day. I don't know what I would do without them. They have been so good to me with everything going on in my life. Also a Happy Father's Day to all the other great dads out there! This day is for you! I will be spending the day at work, another good distraction. Alexa will get to spend the day and celebrate with my parents.

Thursday, June 20th, 2013 at 10:25 pm
Just Another Day

I had yet another doctor's appointment this morning. As usual, after not being there for a while, I had to fill out new paperwork and check off the dreaded widow box. Amazing how that seems so normal to me now. Just another day as a widow!

Saturday, June 22nd, 2013 at 2:02 am
String

"Grief is like a ball of string, you start at one end and wind. Then the ball slips through your fingers and rolls across the floor. Some of your work is undone but not all. You pick it up and start over again, but you never have to begin again at the end of the string. The ball never completely unwinds. You've made some progress."

Today, the ball slipped through my fingers and rolled across the floor. Tomorrow, I pick it up and start again.

Monday, June 24th, 2013 at 1:37 am
Challenges

Each day brings new challenges, new joys, new smiles, and new tears. In that way, my life is no different than anyone else's. We all have hopes and dreams, fears and losses. We all succeed at something and fail at something else. What is important is that we move on from our losses, face our fears, enjoy our successes, learn from our failures, bring on new challenges, and never lose our joy. Someone recently explained to me the difference between happiness and joy. Life circumstances can make you unhappy, but joy is something that lives inside you. It is important to never lose that. And as always, "just keep swimming."

I have interacted with someone recently who was rather unaware of the circumstances of my life until after a few meetings. When she heard about the fact that I was a widow and single mom, and some things that had happened surrounding it, she said, "Wow, you would never know." Of course, I did not have a tape recorder and do not remember the conversation word-for-word, but it was basically stated that I come across as a happy, well-adjusted person and you wouldn't know something terrible had happened to me within the past six months.

I thought about this a lot. I could be miserable and take it out on other people, but where would that get me? Would it bring Alex back? Would it make me happier? No, it certainly would not. Ultimately, in some strange way, I think it may have made me a better person. Don't get me wrong, I don't think I was a bad person and I do not feel that this should have happened to me, but I have learned a lot about myself and others in the past few months. I must also mention that everyone does not see me every minute of every day. I do get angry and upset sometimes. You can tell by my posts.

Recently, more and more people in my life have come forward with stories of people in their lives who have completed suicide. I have conflicting feelings on this. First, I must mention that some of these people I have known for years, and never knew that they were survivors. Now, it is open for conversation as "someone else who can relate." This has happened a lot lately. Others, I do not know well and have come forward looking for someone to talk to in their situation. In general, I am sad to find that so many others know the pain and questioning I do. I appreciate the openness and honesty so much from both the people looking for help and those looking to help me. It is nice to know people care and just as nice to know that I can be of help to people.

Tuesday, June 25th, 2013 at 7:21 pm
Bipolar Disorder

As far as I know, Alex was never officially diagnosed with Bipolar disorder. However, it turns out there is a lot I didn't know. After he passed away, I was told by a family member that it was suspected before we met. Since we did not have much contact with his family at that point, I never knew. I am honestly not sure if he was unaware, denying it, or hiding it from me. I guess I never will. After learning of this, I began researching the disorder.

"Bipolar disorder is a condition in which a person has periods of <u>*depression*</u> *and periods of being extremely happy or being cross or irritable.*

Causes, incidence, and risk factors:

Bipolar disorder affects men and women equally. It usually starts between ages fifteen and twenty-five. The exact cause is not known. But it occurs more often in relatives of people with bipolar disorder.

In most people with bipolar disorder, there is no clear cause for the periods (episodes) of extreme happiness (mania) or depression. The following may trigger a manic episode:

Childbirth

Medicines such as antidepressants or steroids

Periods of not being able to sleep (insomnia)

Recreational drug use

My first thought upon reading this section was "periods of not being able to sleep." At the time of his death, we had a seven-month-old. We had not slept well in a very long time. He was not using drugs, but I did find that he was spending large amounts of money at GNC on weight loss and muscle enhancement supplements. Quite possibly a coincidence, but who knows.

Symptoms

- *The manic phase may last from days to months. It can include these symptoms:*
- *Easily distracted*
- *Little need for sleep*
- *Poor judgment*
- *Poor temper control*
- *Reckless behavior and lack of self control such as drinking, drug use, sex with many partners, spending sprees*
- *Very elevated, expansive or irritable mood, such as racing thoughts, talking a lot, false beliefs about self or abilities*
- *Very involved in activities*

Alex was one of the most easily distracted people I have ever met in my life. We used to both joke and fight about it. He could be carrying a fifty pound litter box, walk past the TV, notice the TV, and forget what he was doing. He would be able to just stand there holding the litter, completely lost in what was on TV.

Having a conversation could be difficult at times, as he would get distracted by the slightest thing. His sleep patterns always amazed me. He would go through periods where he would be up half the night playing video games and seemed fine. Other times, he wanted to go to bed at 6 pm. He did have poor judgment with certain things, but I never felt it was anything out of control.

As far as reckless behaviors are concerned, he was very reckless with money. Other than that, he was not. He had NO temper control toward the end. This did not seem to be an issue when we met. As time went on, it would get worse and worse. He would punch things, say crazy things, threaten, scream at me to get away because he can't control himself, etc. Five minutes later, he was back to his happy self. Very involved in activities is an understatement. If you look through these, a lot can describe anyone. I really just thought it was his personality.

The depressive episode may include these symptoms:

- *Daily low mood or sadness*
- *Difficulty concentrating, remembering, or making decisions*
- *Eating problems such as loss of appetite and weight loss, or overeating and weight gain*
- *Fatigue or lack of energy*
- *Feeling worthless, hopeless, or guilty*
- *Loss of pleasure in activities once enjoyed*
- *Loss of self-esteem*
- *Thoughts of death or suicide*
- *Trouble getting to sleep or sleeping too much*
- *Pulling away from friends or activities that were once enjoyed*

Looking back, I see pretty much all of these. He would go through phases of sadness. Don't we all? We fought a lot about him not remembering things. I would have a vivid recollection of a conversation that he said we never had. I was told a lot that I did not keep him informed when I felt I did.

Over the years, he lost weight, gained weight, lost weight, gained weight. But so did I! The amount of energy he had amazed me sometimes. Other times, he was too tired to do anything. He always lost pleasure in activities. Something he once loved, he suddenly didn't care about anymore. It would be replaced by something else. He would get very down on himself and say he didn't know what I saw in him.

As I mentioned, sleep was always a weird thing for him. I learned a lot that he used to hide behind me to not have to hang out with friends. He was doing this in the end. He would say I had to work, or he would ask me and then never respond. Clearly, he was suicidal, as we all know the end result.

Persons with bipolar disorder are at high risk of suicide. They may abuse alcohol or other substances. This can make the symptoms and suicide risk worse. At least 25% to 50% of patients with bipolar disorder attempt suicide at least once.

Episodes of depression are more common than episodes of mania. The pattern is not the same in all persons with bipolar disorder:

Depression and mania symptoms may occur together. This is called a mixed state.

Symptoms may also occur right after each other. This is called rapid cycling.

I'm not even sure how to explain it, but this makes sense to me. I think in the rapid cycling or mixed state, it makes it harder to notice. Does any of this mean anything now? Probably not. It certainly won't bring him back. Still, I maybe feel a slight bit of relief or a sense of some questions answered. It backs up my feelings that HE didn't do this, his mind did.

Friday, June 28th, 2013 at 2:36 am
Tomorrow

Tomorrow, I am going to my friend's wedding. Right now, I am very excited. I am looking forward to getting dressed up and having a night out. I am taking my married, female cousin as a date. I know we will have a blast together. It is time for me to start doing normal things again and start learning how to move on. This is my life and it is not going to change, so I'd better get used to it.

That being said, I know there may be some rough moments tomorrow. Alex won't be there when a slow love song comes on and he will not be running around with his camera as the photographer. Neither will I. I'm just going to go, relax, and have fun. I don't need the reminder of taking photos alone.

I was just thinking today how funny it is that five years later, I'm going to the wedding of the woman who caught my bouquet! In talking about it today, I actually referred to myself as single. A friend mentioned that she thought that was a big step for me. I still think it's a technicality. I don't know that I will be comfortable enough to try to catch hers, but I won't 100% count it out yet. Every day of my life is happy and sad at the same time. Tomorrow will be too.

Way back when, I wrote about how I kept hearing that song that should have been our wedding song. Every event we went to, we always missed dancing to it. After he died, I got very angry hearing it and screamed at him. I never heard it again. Interestingly enough, I heard it twice today. I feel like he's trying to tell me something. I just don't know what. I'm ready to see what tomorrow will bring!

Saturday, June 29th, 2013 at 10:56 pm
There I Was...

Ready for a wedding? The ceremony began. The bride looked so beautiful. I started to tear up and then could not control my crying. I was crying so much that I had to get up and walk out. Not a good way to start the day, but I was hoping this would get it all out. We had some time in between, so went to a friend's house to hang out for a bit. It was nice to relax and catch up. Time went by fast and I was ready to have some fun.

Cocktail hour was a blast. I enjoyed my one wedding cake martini and spending time with my friends. I was confident it was going to be a great night. The hour went by quickly and it was time to go into the reception. It was so beautiful and I was surrounded by friends. Again, I was ready to do this!

The introductions were great and I was really getting into it. The next thing I heard was, "And now the bride and groom will dance their first dance to 'From This Moment' by Shania Twain." I turned to my table and said, "This is MY wedding song," and ran out the door, down the hall and outside, as quickly as possible. I did not want to get upset again and I knew I could not watch someone else dance to this song.

My cousin and my friend chased me down the hall in high heels. Thinking back, this must have been a hilarious sight. I got through it without a tear, or hearing the song, and went back in. Things got fun. When the first slow song came on, a good friend danced with me. Thankfully, his wife is a good friend too and she didn't mind. I don't even know what song it was, but it meant a lot that someone cared and he did not think twice about just grabbing my hand and taking me to the dance floor.

The fast songs came on and I danced and sang and had a blast. One of Alex's favorite songs was "Sweet Caroline." I danced and sang my ass off, all the while thinking, "This one's for you baby." Things were going great when they showed a slideshow of photos the photographers had taken earlier in the day. They were beautiful. Watching, I started thinking of our days of wedding photography together and again, burst into tears. I was so mad at myself. I felt like I made an ass of myself and made other people uncomfortable at the table. Everyone assured me it was fine and they were all missing him too. I'm still disappointed that I could not have a normal night out without getting upset.

With all of this going on, I went to the ladies' room at just the right time and missed having to actually say no to going up for the bouquet. I know I am single, but I just do not feel comfortable with all of that. I am glad I was not involved. I calmed down, had some dessert, and started getting back into the swing of things.

Towards the end of the night, "Amazed" by Lonestar came on. That song being the one I have described before. Our song that we always miss and now I keep hearing again. My cousin asked what I wanted to do, leave, dance, etc. Another friend said he would dance with me. It worked out well and I felt better about it. Again, thankful his wife was okay with that.

Just to make things funnier, as I was leaving, I saw a bride from another wedding. She was wearing my wedding dress! Well not mine, but the same dress! I just had to laugh by this point. The day had some major ups and downs, but I am glad I went. I would have been upset if I missed it. It was a big step, and even though I did not get through it with flying colors, I got through it. I know people are proud of me and I should be too. I'm trying. Huge thanks to everyone who got me through the night!

Sunday, June 30th, 2013 at 3:13 pm
Back to "Normal"

Today was back to normal. I spent the night alone in my house for the first time. It was rather uneventful. Alexa and I were both so tired and went to bed very early. Not much else to say about that.

July 2013

Tuesday, July 1st, 2013 at 12:20 am
Cuz I'm Halfway There

Yesterday was officially six months without Alex. It was a normal day at work (as normal as my job is). I felt as though it was a depressing day, but was reminded that I should be proud of making it this far. All I can say is, "Yup, I'm still breathing." They say it gets easier after a year. I'm halfway there. This is also the week leading up to his birthday. On Saturday, Alex would have turned thirty. I will still be celebrating his life this weekend.

It seems as though as soon as I'm doing okay, something kicks me back down. I have been doing well overall. This week, I feel like I'm falling apart again in dealing with the anniversary and his birthday. Depression is trying to take over. I'd like to spend most of the time in bed and eat whatever I want, but I won't.

Wednesday, July 3rd, 2013 at 11:15pm
Roses are Red, White, and Blue?

I used to say that buying flowers was a waste. They are expensive and just die anyway. Today, I saw a red, white, and blue dyed rose. I just wanted it. I justified it to myself by saying that it should survive until Friday and can go to the grave. Looking at it now, I realize that for some reason, it just makes me feel good. It's beautiful and I need some beauty in my world.

Tomorrow is a holiday that we would usually spend

together and spend celebrating Alex's birthday. Instead, I will be working. I think that's a good idea. Like I always say, it's a normal busy day that keeps my mind off of things. Friday, I will decorate his grave and finish my shopping for his party. I'm looking forward to spending his actual birthday surrounded by people I love, and not alone. It was a long day today and I'm tired. Tonight, I'm wishing I could hear him say he's proud of me. As crazy as it is, I have a really hard time remembering his voice. That really bothers me!

Sunday, July 7th, 2013 at 11:13 pm
Happy Birthday, Alex

My first post was about a support group. Although it was not really a positive experience for me, I did come out with something. Someone mentioned the importance of their life, not their death and therefore the day of their birth, not their death. This weekend, we did just that.

Alex would have turned thirty on Saturday. I spent the extended three day weekend surrounded by friends and family celebrating him. Like anything, there were great moments and bad, but I got through it surrounded by wonderful people whom Alex meant a lot to, who are special to me, and can relate. I'm sad to see everyone leave and life go back to normal. The stages of grief went full circle and more this weekend. Details to follow.

Wednesday, July 10th, 2013 at 12:45 pm
Weekend Recap

I'm finally getting a chance to write the real weekend update. I've been getting life back to normal and haven't had much time. Friday began with a trip to see Alex. I decorated his grave for his birthday. The strange thing about it is I didn't get upset. I didn't really feel anything. As terrible as it sounds, it felt more like an obligatory visit. I had to do it, so I did.

The day was filled with preparations for the weekend. I needed to shop and the house needed to be cleaned. Of course, I still ended up with multiple Walmart visits. Friends started to arrive that night. I was so excited to see them and that's all that mattered. Saturday morning arrived and as usual, I started to feel like I really didn't want to do this. I didn't have a choice anymore. People were on their way. I felt like I would have much rather ignored the day instead of celebrated, but I knew it would be okay.

The worst part of everything was the cake. Picking it up, I felt like I was going to vomit right there in Walmart. Thankfully, I didn't. Later in the day came the question of what do I do with it? Do I silently cut it up? Should we sing? We collectively decided to take that time to let people say anything they wanted. I tried to get out, "I love you, I miss you," but burst into tears and had to walk away. I guess that had to happen once this weekend.

We spent the weekend telling stories and just remembering him. We all have amazing memories of him. I have to say, it seems as though the best part of the weekend was the Slip 'N Slide. Who would've thought? I can only imagine crazy Alex throwing himself through it. I know he would have!

Sunday afternoon, people started to clear out and my headache started to get out of control. I shouldn't be surprised. I ate things I shouldn't have, drank a little, barely slept, and was out in the sun all weekend. I took a nap and went back to the graveyard. I wanted to see the lights and candles in the dark.

This visit was very different. This time I was there because I wanted to be. I laid in the grass with him and just cried and cried. I was such a mess. I didn't want to leave and thought I'd have to be dragged out of there. Thankfully, the storm took care of that for me.

All in all, I spent the weekend surrounded by people I care about who care about me. That is exactly what I needed. Every night was spent out on the deck talking. Monday night was sad when no one was here anymore. They may not be here, but I know everyone is just a phone call away.

Tuesday, July 23rd, 2013 at 10:41 pm
You Never Know

It's always the things you aren't prepared for that knocks your legs out from under you and sends you into tears. For me anyway. There are always things that I am prepared for and things that I expect may upset me. I'm learning that this isn't going to change yet.

This weekend, Alexa and I were in New Jersey celebrating a first birthday. Saturday was the family party, which I was asked to attend and photograph. Sunday was the friend party, at which we were guests. I expected that going to a party where I would be surrounded by couples and families would be upsetting. Interestingly enough, it wasn't. Alexa is my family and that's all I needed. I expected that seeing acquaintances that I hadn't seen in a long time would be awkward, considering my new life. It wasn't. I always expected people to assume that Alexa was adopted and when someone actually said it to me (surprisingly for the first time), it was actually funny, not upsetting.

I was terrified at the thought of photographing an event without Alex, but it really wasn't all that scary. I did not get the joy out of it that I used to and my photos certainly aren't as good as his, but that's okay. The point is, I did it, and I got through it.

I knew bringing my cousin with me to events opened us to looking like a lesbian couple with a child. I did not expect this to upset me, and it didn't. I think it's pretty funny that someone actually asked.

What I did NOT expect at a one-year-old's party was to overhear a loud conversation about mentally ill people legally accessing guns because background checks do not include mental health checks, thus they become a menace to society. I froze and politely excused myself from the room. I then burst into tears. I'm not sure how I should have handled the situation, but I'm mad that I handled it that way. This event was not about me and I had a breakdown right in the middle. I guess it's just one more thing I had to experience. You live and you learn. Otherwise, it was a good weekend. It is just nice to get away and be surrounded by friends sometimes.

Wednesday, July 31st, 2013 at 1:48 am
Remember Me

I struggle to find something to watch on TV at night, knowing that something simple can send me in a downward spiral of depression or rage. I searched and searched for something to watch and finally chose "Remember Me" for the sheer fact that I like Robert Pattinson. I probably should have researched a bit first because apparently the description clearly states it is about death and suicide. It was a good movie, but put me back in the dark place and left me in tears for the night. Oops. Lesson learned: don't pick a movie just because the actor looks hot with a beat-up face.

One thing I took away from the movie was how he always wrote his deceased brother letters. I decided to do this today. I wrote what I was feeling and needed to get out, and I left it at his grave. Here is what I wrote:

"I'm sick of hating you. I'm sick of loving you. I hate that you did this to us. I hate that I spend my days defending you. You said I always had to get in the last word. You really took that away, didn't you? I can live my life without you. But why should I have to? Was it worth it? Really? Buying stuff behind my back, going places behind my back. Was it worth dying? I don't know how to stop loving you, but it sure would make my life easier if I could. Your daughter will never know you, and it's your fault, but I am the one that worries about it. You left me with wounds that will never heal and scars that will forever damage me. I wish you could take it back. I would forgive everything and we could start again. I can't ever hug you again and that still doesn't make sense to me. Instead I'll just lay here and stare at your stone. I'll never find someone like you."

August 2013

Monday, August 5th, 2013 at 2:52 am
All Over a New Phone

This is my first post from my new phone. Getting this phone was such a pain in my ass today! I felt like I had to keep jumping through hoops to figure out how to do it. I have been putting it off for a while, a long while, mainly because of the fear of losing three years' worth of Alex's texts.

Yesterday, my old phone got a black screen and suddenly stopped working. I finally got it working and it seemed as though all of my texts had mysteriously vanished. I couldn't believe it. Someone told me maybe it was a sign that Alex was telling me to move on. Of course, that made me cry and then just as quickly as they disappeared, they came back. I'm not sure what happened but somehow, I clicked the text icon for probably the fifth time and there they were.

I still decided to get a new phone. I did all my research on transferring my texts, and still, I can't figure out how to get them on this new phone. *Sigh* Maybe it isn't that important. I still have the old phone. It's not like I read them anyway. How often do you want to read the last text that says, "Mow, you're scaring me"? I guess I'll sleep on it and decide if I've given up or I'm going to keep researching and keep trying.

Thursday, August 8th, 2013 at 2:41 am
Fatherless Children

I saw this statistic online about US children who come from fatherless homes.

"90% of all runaways
80% have behavioral disorders
71% of teenage pregnancies"

It breaks my heart to think Alexa falls into the category of fatherless children. It sounds so strange to me. She has a father, well had, I guess. She is just not being raised by one. Sometimes I think I worry about her future too much. I know that is my job as a mom, but what is too much? I have no experience in this department. I grew up with two parents. What is it like to grow up with just one?

I will do my best to be a mother and a father, but I know that is not ideal. I can't change it and I can't drive myself nuts worrying about it. I guess all I can do is be the best mom I know how to be. I hope someday she can look back with fond memories of her childhood and be proud of me. I think that may be my biggest goal in life now. I want to be someone that my daughter is proud of.

Monday, August 12th, 2013 at 1:27 am
The Things I Needed to Say

I spent the last four days in a very intense seminar about The Grief Recovery Method. It has been a very emotional few days. I am surrounded by amazing people and right now, cannot even put into words what I gained from this experience. Some of the little things that have happened there have been so powerful for me. At the conclusion of the workshop, I had to write a letter of all the words that were left unspoken. It was so easy to write, yet so hard to read. Here it is:

"Mom, I have been reviewing our relationship and discovered some things I want to say. Mom, I am sorry I did not know to get you help. I should have been paying closer attention. I am sorry I did not realize what you were telling me that day. I should not have let my anger get in the way of making sure you were safe. I am sorry I couldn't save you. I would have done anything. I am sorry I said all the wrong things. I should have shut up and told you how much I love you, instead of continuing the argument. I will forever be sorry that was the last communication we had. I am sorry you did not know I wouldn't have left you. At that moment, I knew I would not have. I'm sorry I didn't tell you that. I'm sorry I thought you were making excuses for your actions. I should have realized you really were *trying to find answers about your behaviors. Mom, I forgive you for ending your life. I know you did not do it to hurt me. I know you thought you were doing the right thing. I know you were sick and couldn't see the effects clearly. I forgive you for your anger and violent spells. I know that wasn't the real you. I forgive you for smoking. I know I'm a hypocrite now since I started smoking again. I forgive you for not always saying or doing what I felt was appropriate. Even though I still don't understand why you did the things you did, I forgive you. Mom, I want you to know that I do know that you truly loved me. I want you to know that you forever changed the woman I am. I want you to know that I recognize that I'm not perfect and I've made mistakes too. I want you to know that Alexa will always be a wonderful gift the you gave me. you will always hold a piece of my heart. I miss you so much. I love you. Goodbye."*

Wednesday, August 14th, 2013 at 1:08 am
Dada

I've always worried about explaining the daddy thing. By always, obviously I mean since he's been gone. I was not sure how I felt about Alexa going to the cemetery. I had decided that I would always tell the truth. I don't believe in lying to Alexa and figured I would tell her as much as I thought she could handle. How much can a fourteen-month-old really understand? More than I realize, I think. I feel that if I am always open about it, it will be normal to her and less likely to be an issue later.

I have a tendency to go visit Alex after my chiropractor appointment. Alexa usually falls asleep in the car after her adjustment. I usually pull up next to his stone and leave the truck running. This way she can sleep in the car while I sit with him. Today was a different story. We had a cranky day. I can't really pinpoint why, but it was a day of tantrums and I just had a hard time keeping her happy. She usually loves car rides. Again, today was different.

Pulling into the cemetery, she was screaming. Certainly not going to fall asleep at this point. I was not sure what to do. I knew she wouldn't sit quietly in the car while I visited. So, I got past the trepidation of letting her walk around the graveyard. I took her out of the car and she walked up to his grave. Alexa's favorite phrase right now is, "What's that?" Really it sounds like, "Dat?" Seriously one of the cutest sounds I've ever heard.

Not surprisingly, she pointed to the stone and said, "Dat?" I responded simply by saying it was a stone. Again, "Dat?" I pointed to his photo on the stone and said, "That's daddy." She stared at the photo and said, "Dada." I told her she was right and said this is where we come to see and talk to dada. She said, "Hi daddy." I said, "Alexa do you understand?" She stood there staring (can you believe a toddler stood still) and said, "Yeah."

Now how much of what I was saying did she really understand? I don't know. But it did give me a sense of relief. She pointed to his flowers and asked again what they were. I told her they were daddy's flowers. Soon she started pointing to everything she saw and asking, "Dat? Dat? Dat?" I finally said, "Alexa, there are other people here too." I really think I was just searching for something to say and that's all I could come up with. She got quiet and began to wander around. I kept telling her we had to walk back to daddy. She would take my hand and follow me back.

Although I never got to sit there and relax and say what I wanted to say, it was a good experience. I think it was the happiest she was all day. How much of that did she understand? Probably not as much as it seemed, but who knows.

Friday, August 23rd, 2013 at 2:25 am
Am I Angry?

Recently, I was asked if all the changes I needed to make in my life make me angry. I simply responded, "No, I'm not angry." Anger is a normal part of the grieving process and even more prevalent in cases of suicide.

Looking back at old posts, I was clearly VERY angry. The feeling would come and go. I think I can finally say I've let it go. It is time to move on from the anger. I previously discussed going through the grief recovery training and discussed how I was able to let it all go. There are answers I will never get and that's okay. There are things I will never understand and that's okay. I finally accept that Alex did what he thought was right in the moment. Irrational or not, he thought what he was doing was right. Yes, I wrote that twice. I need to no longer be angry for that. I finally feel that I'm there. I've made it to acceptance. This is my life and I can't do anything but move forward.

Without all the pain or anger, I can finally just breathe and miss him. I am making a lot of positive life changes right now. I'm taking calculated risks to better my life, Alexa's life, and others around me. There has been a lot of stress associated with it, but I believe it will all be worth it.

I believe Alex is watching and cheering me on. I know he still wants what is best for me. I would rather him be here to stand by and be proud, but I'll take what I can get. Although I will never truly find the positivity in his death, I am doing my best to make something good out of it. As always, I love and miss you Mow and I hope I'm doing the right things.

Saturday, August 24th, 2013 at 2:14 am
100%

It's interesting how it seems that when I find myself in a positive place, I fall back down the very next day. I had a lot planned for the weekend and as usual, was semi-looking forward to it. I say semi because it always takes a lot for me to get myself geared up and going, but when I actually do it, I am glad I did.

Two of my friends are celebrating their birthdays on the Jersey shore and I was going to bring Alexa to the beach for the first time. I was nervous about having a toddler at the beach and all that entails, but I wanted to see everyone and couldn't wait to see the first time she put her feet in the sand. Knowing I couldn't spend the whole day there, I planned to go visit some family after and spend the night. I don't see them enough and couldn't wait to get there and catch up. I planned to attempt to stop in at another party on Sunday where Alexa could hang out with some kids her age. I don't have enough playdates with her.

She has been fighting what seems to be a stomach virus this week and had seemed to get better. Today, while I was at work, she got sick again. Knowing I had to cancel my trip really got to me. I suddenly realized how much I wanted to go and began to cry. I knew that it is not about me, but what was best for her. I cried even more, feeling selfish for being upset in the first place.

I don't do well with normal weekends. Being home with nothing more to do than my usual chores reminds me that he is gone and I fall into a depression every time. Just knowing that this weekend had the potential to be that had the depression starting already. I wondered how it would have been different if Alex were still here. Well for one thing, he may have been able to stay home with her so I could at least go see my friends for a bit and come home. Or, he would have been here to spend the weekend home with me.

This also brought out the realization of just how far away my friends are. I can't just run out really quickly to see them. There is a plan, a long drive, and a whole production to figure out just for a few hours with them. It seems as though the huge things that should upset me don't, but the little things, such as a weekend change, set me off.

It was a long day and a long week and I'm exhausted. Alex would have known how to make me feel better, whether it was with a smile or a Wawa sub or a cute note. I went and got the Wawa sub on my own. It wasn't the same, but it was pretty good. It comes down to the fact that to me, this is a loss, and every loss is grieved at one hundred percent.

Sunday, August 25th, 2013 at 8:20 pm
Think Before You Speak!

Yesterday, I found myself in a conversation with a good friend of mine. A woman that I vaguely know entered the conversation and proceeded to tell me that she feels my pain because due to work, her husband was only home on weekends for a few months. She commented that she knew what being a single mom was like because that's the same thing. I was so shocked that the only words I could muster up were, "Being a widow with a fifteen-month-old is hard." This ended the conversation.

My mind is still reeling. Does someone really think this is the same thing? My husband is dead, not in the next state. I can't call him when I'm frustrated, upset, missing him, or need advice. He is not coming home in a few days. My child is not away from her father for a little while. He's gone. I have to take care of her without her dad while I grieve his death.

This is NOT the same thing. Why do we feel the need to act as though something we have been through makes us understand? There is no way to ever understand what someone else is feeling. Even if I met another widow from suicide with a child, I still may not understand or feel their pain. No two situations are the same.

This reminds me of a prior incident. Someone recently told me they miss Alex as much as I do. I was so upset and hurt that I could not even form coherent thoughts to respond. I have no idea what their former relationship was, but I can say that in the last ten years, there wasn't one. This person was not a part of our lives. My world was broken. The love of my life, man I shared my life with, and father of my child died. I will never fully recover and never be the same. I relive finding him and struggle with everyday activities that I used to take for granted. And you miss him as much as I do? Tell me, how has your life changed? I'm sure this person meant well and was trying to be nice. I do. But it came across as rude and insensitive.

People that I spend a fairly decent amount of time with will still comment that they want to "blow their brains out." People still think it is okay to look right at me and mimic shooting themselves in the head to announce that they are frustrated.

You would think that people don't need another reminder to think before you speak (or type), but I learn every day that we do.

Thursday, August 29th, 2013 at 11:55 pm
Here We Go Again!

Here we go again. I've been making a big effort to move on. I don't mean run out and find a new husband. I mean come to terms with being single and attempt to enjoy life on my own. I've been making changes with myself and my life. I'm becoming more comfortable with everything. I'm living on my own and supporting myself. I'm able to enjoy memories now without falling apart every time. I'm parting with more of Alex's belongings that I have no reason to keep. I have still maintained letting go of the anger. I'm happy with the progress I am making. I'm not in a funk anymore, I think. I'm cooking more, doing my schoolwork, starting new endeavors, and enjoying every new experience with Alexa.

I had a long day today and was looking forward to relaxing tonight and starting a new day tomorrow. I have a lot planned for my day off. I came home and went on Facebook. I try very hard to avoid letting myself get frustrated with what I see. I could not help myself and got involved in a conversation in which someone I do not know referred to suicide as "taking the selfish forever fifth" and then went on to say it is an admission of guilt and makes you a monster.

My blood is boiling. I am shaking. I know this is not directed at me nor Alex, but I am so hurt. My husband was not a monster. He was a sick man whom chose the wrong path. I never want to think of him that way. Why do we, as a society, judge and automatically decide someone is a terrible person for one action, one mistake in life? Does nothing else he did with his life matter? So I'm up at almost midnight, cooking. Not for me. I will not be eating this meal. I am not sure why chopping vegetables was my attempt at getting out my anger. It helped a bit. Now I'm left here alone and upset. I should not let an ignorant comment keep me awake, but it is. I'm so sick of it all. I'm really trying to just let it go and move on. Something will always jump up and get in my way. I can't let it.

Saturday, August 31st, 2013 at 11:04 pm
Today Sucked

Today sucked. That pretty much explains it all. Today is eight months. Eight months since my life completely changed and I lost my best friend. Somehow the months that have a 31st day always seem to feel worse.

It started last night when I laid in bed replaying the events of the night of his death. I didn't know why I was doing it again, but couldn't help it. I attempted to have a normal day, but everything hit me hard. I'm usually able to handle crying clients, but it started to get to me today and I cried too.

I met another widow today. It has been over four years for her. She told me that it never gets easier. You just learn to work through it. That makes sense. A setback in my work schedule change had me in tears yet again. I couldn't completely calm down for hours. I cried more, knowing all these changes came from one night that totally revamped my life.

I'm just in a funk tonight. I got home hoping to relax and play with Alexa, only to find the neighbors setting off fireworks right behind me. It was loud and kept scaring me. I jump easily now. The dogs were freaking out. Alexa was getting upset. This is not how I wanted to spend my night. So all I can really say is today sucked. Tomorrow is another day.

September 2013

Sunday, September 8th, 2013 at 1:42 am
Words

I spend a lot of time writing. I get out a lot of my feelings here and am truly documenting my journey. I used to go back and read what I had previously written over and over. I don't really know why. This blog has gotten long and to go back and read everything would certainly be time consuming. Though I hope that new readers do go back and read my journey, I don't really need to do it all the time.

Imagine my surprise when I received a message from a reader that the blog was gone. How could that be? Hacked? Why would someone do that? Being previously married to an IT guy, you would think I have backups. Funny thing about that, I don't. Well, I do now. Suddenly, my entire journey was gone and I didn't know if I would ever get it back. Clearly, I did, but at the time, I didn't know that.

The site was gone, but I was still able to see the posts in my WordPress app. In a little under two hours, I went into each post, copied it, and emailed it to myself. I was so thankful for my iPhone. It was like 220 emails! I just kept thinking I had to keep going, as fast as I could, in case I got locked out. After every few, I would find one and think, "This is a good one, need this one!"

I was panicking thinking about the fact that so much of the book I plan to write relies on the feelings I have written, in the moment I was feeling them. I can't get that back! I never realized how much this meant to me. This was a true testament of not knowing what you have until it's gone.

I told a friend that my entire life the past eight months was in this blog. It is so true. I'm so thankful to have these words I have written. They are typed on my phone most of the time. I learned my lesson. BACKUP your work! Not that I consider this work, but you know. This pushed me to realize how much I want to write my book. I will do it.

Tuesday, September 10th, 2013 at 11:31 pm
Suicide Awareness and Prevention Day

Well here it is, the post I have been thinking about all day. Today is Suicide Awareness and Prevention day. I expected a normal day and woke up feeling not-so-normal. I knew I would light a candle at 8 pm tonight since it was all over Twitter to do that in remembrance. I invited everyone else to do the same and posted it as well. I flooded Twitter and Facebook announcing what today was. I knew I would write about it tonight.

I kept thinking about awareness for others, but seeing all of those candles with Alex's name really hit me hard. I cried and cried that this wasn't about statistics and being helpful. This was about losing the man I love to something that should have been prevented. I've learned a lot about myself and suicide statistics and facts over the past eight months. But no matter what, he's not coming back.

I read post after post of people who thought about or attempted suicide and are thankful to have survived. I know he would have been. Suicide is such a hush hush issue and it needs to be brought to light. I'm glad we have a week like this to do it.

Thank you so much to my friends and family who posted photos of their lit candles. I cannot tell you how much that meant to me. Even though I cried, I had my amazing little girl to wipe my tears and give me a hug. I don't know what I would do without her. Outside things in my life made this a rough day to begin with, and this made it harder. That's okay. Today is not about me. It is about raising awareness and saving someone else. I made it through and tomorrow is another day. A day that will be so difficult for so many other people out there.

Friday, September 21st, 2013 at 10:31 pm
In Preparation

Tomorrow is another big yard sale day. I've done one before, so selling Alex's items isn't new to me. Nothing had me in tears but there were certainly some thought provoking moments. The day before his death, Alex and I played Guitar Hero for the first time in years. When we started dating, we played constantly! We had Guitar Hero parties at our house and had hours of fun.

Over the weekend before his death, we discussed how we did not have the same hobbies or interests anymore. I was still interested in photography, but he wasn't. World of Warcraft did not interest him anymore and he had moved into Call of Duty. Shooting games give me anxiety. Though it was winter, I was looking forward to nice weather to start cycling again, but he wanted to sell his bike. I spent nights online couponing and researching babies, while he played video games and looked at comics. He wanted me to go to the gun range and I refused.

That weekend, we spent time together watching old movies, playing with Alexa, and playing Guitar Hero for old times' sake. We had so much fun! Today, I decided it was time to sell the Guitar Hero guitars and drums. I'm not going to play by myself. There's no need for them to sit here collecting dust. I couldn't help but think about all of our times playing, especially our last time.

I posted the yard sale on numerous sites, listing some of the things I was selling. Someone messaged me asking what size men's clothes I was selling. Nine months ago, I would have known his exact clothing size. Today, I had no idea. I had to go look. I'm starting to forget details about him, and that scares me.

There is still so much stuff in my basement. I'm finding old car parts, papers, and just random crap. Some of this are things we just never unpacked when we moved three years ago. Some is from before we even met. I find myself asking him what the hell to do with it all, and asking him to direct me toward stuff I could actually sell. I think he was there helping. I hope he was there helping.

Sunday, September 22nd, 2013 at 12:41 am
Long Day

Today has been a very long day. I couldn't sleep last night. I found myself wandering my house wondering if this is what insomnia feels like. I finally found myself getting sleepy at 12:15 this morning. Alexa woke up crying at 12:30 am. I got her back to sleep (stupid night terrors) and probably was asleep a little after 1 am. Before I knew it, it was 5 am and the alarm was going off.

It was yard sale day. I was at my parents and unpacking by 6 am. People started arriving before I even finished. I had a lot to sell and wanted it all gone. I did well. Something about watching someone walk away with Alex's work boots really got me. I'm not sure why that one item bothered me, but it stopped me in my tracks. I had to get back into the moment and continue selling. I'm happy that his items are being put to use and not ending up as trash.

Since I couldn't shop and I love yard sales, my mom and Alexa went out shopping for me. They came back with a photo of a swing set someone was selling. I ran to look at it and decided to buy it. We finished the yard sale and packed everything back up.

My dad and I headed to take apart the swing set and bring it to my house. Standing there watching him with his tools, I was thankful that I had him to help me, but knew it should be Alex doing it. I finally blurted out, "We are both thinking it so I'm just going to say it. This would be easier if Alex were here." I have been very determined to leave my anger behind, but felt it sneaking in today.

He is supposed to be here to do this for his daughter! He was young, strong, and great with tools. He would have had this figured out in no time. He should be sharing the excitement of his daughter's first swing set! I decided to let the anger go and just feel sorry that he couldn't be here to enjoy this. We got it done. Well, I didn't do much, but it's done. Just as we expected, Alexa saw it and immediately asked, "What's that?" It was a long day on four hours of sleep. I'm exhausted and sitting outside watching the rain while a visiting frog watches me write. Let's hope I fall asleep as quickly as Alexa did.

Saturday, September 28th, 2013 at 2:21 am
TV

I've noticed that the way I react to movies and TV shows has changed over the past almost nine months. I don't necessarily mean this in a bad way, but life experiences make you view things differently. I do not watch a lot of TV shows. I pretty much only religiously follow "Grey's Anatomy." I love this show, but something about last night's episode bothered me. A woman arrived at the hospital right after her husband passed away. She was crying. In this case, I did not feel her pain. I questioned her reaction. Was my experience different than others or was this inaccurate?

For me, I could not cry. Even wanting and trying to, I physically could not. Being in shock, my body would not allow it.

I understood what was going on, but was literally in a daze and could not feel anything. I stayed in this daze for days. I functioned as best as possible, but as far as I can remember, I did not cry until walking into the funeral home for the private viewing. The days are a blur, so I can't be positive it was that long, but still. To me, that scene seemed so unrealistic. Your body literally protects you from falling apart in a crisis situation.

I stayed up late a few nights ago watching some stupid movie that I don't even remember the name of. I knew the movie was dumb but I needed to know the ending! Toward the end, the main couple were seemingly breaking up and the woman stated, "I cannot live without him." I wanted to scream at the TV. You CAN live without him. You just don't want to. I can live without Alex and I am. I just don't want to.

Sunday, September 29th, 2013 at 12:31am
Out of the Darkness 5K

Today was the Dover Out of the Darkness Suicide Prevention walk. What an experience. When I signed up for the walk, I decided this would be an opportunity for me to connect with others in the area and share my story. Since there was a resource fair, I decided to have a table for the blog. Recently, we were invited to bring a pair of shoes to commemorate our loved ones. They were to be placed along the path of the walk, then donated to a homeless shelter afterwards. I picked out a pair of Alex's shoes to bring with me.

I woke up early this morning and got there to set up my table. I met a lot of amazing people today. What hit me the most was looking around and realizing that all of these people had been affected by suicide in some way. We all have the same goal: to prevent this from happening to someone else and to end the silence! Talk about your experience! Open up and get the stigma removed. These are all amazing people that just needed some help. Help is out there and we need to make that known. This blog is my way of doing that.

The beginning of the 5K was hard and I cried my way through the first few blocks. I'm not sure what hit me, but I had to get it out. Seeing Alex's shoes along the path brought such an indescribable feeling. I wanted to just stop there and stand there with him. I wanted to steal them back. I have gotten rid of so many of his things, so why were these shoes different? Today, they had meaning. They represented his presence. I took photos and moved on.

It was a beautiful walk. Alexa did great! I think she had fun! When we arrived at the finish line, she was asleep in the stroller. I think the excitement got to her. I am so thankful for my friends and family who walked with me and for those who donated. I raised $500 and the walk raised $36,000! Today was great and today was hard, but I did it, and I'm glad I did.

October 2013

Thursday, October 3rd, 2013 at 2:19 am
The Past is Never Far

One of the computers at work got a pretty impressive virus today. It actually stated that the FBI had noted illegal activity and had been recording the computer. It froze and asked for money to unfreeze it. Seems legit, right? I couldn't help but wish I could show Alex. He would have certainly gotten a kick out of it, being an IT administrator. Watching our admin remote login and work on the computer bothered me, as Alex used to remote login to my computer at home. It almost felt like he was the one on the other side making my mouse move.

I have officially been at my job for three years. It is time for my yearly review. My boss brought me my self-evaluation and last year's review for reference. I froze and felt sick. I don't want to think about the past year. Life was so different then.

One year ago, I had recently come back from maternity leave. Life was good. Now, I'm a different person. My head is in a fog. My focus is surviving each day and getting through to the next. In my own world, that's how it feels, even though it may not seem that way. Each day, I look forward to saying that I did it, I made it through one more day without him. I did what I could to find some joy in the day.

More than once I have been told that the second year is worse and that the first anniversary is horrible. I still have a few months to go and I'm starting to get scared. Is this true?

Tuesday, October 8th, 2013 at 1:07 pm
A Room Full of Widows

9 am and it's been interesting already. I made an appointment to get the oil changed on my truck for first thing in the morning. I will be leaving for vacation this weekend and it needed to be done before the long drive. I pulled into the place and started getting Alexa in her stroller. Employees immediately walked up and started getting set up. A woman was standing nearby and said, "Miss Lobby?" Somehow, I didn't even realize she was talking to me.

She came closer and said, "You're Miss Lobby, right?" The truck is in my dad's name, so I totally understood the assumption, but still. I told her that yes, this is the truck but that's not my name. It shouldn't bother me, but I am still Mrs. and I deserve that title.

My name is Cruz and will stay that way. I'm not divorced, I'm widowed. Cruz is the name I relate to. No big deal. She didn't know, but it got me thinking nonetheless.

I walked into the little waiting room carrying my diaper bag and pushing Alexa in a stroller. There were three elderly women in the room. Looking up at me, one said, "Gee I guess none of our husbands take care of our cars for us." I just blurted out, "I'm widowed, so no." She responded that she is too. I wondered where the comment came from then. The two other women looked up and said, "Me too." She responded with, "Wow, we are a room full of widows." Silence.

After a minute, she looked at me and said, "But you're so young." I never know how to respond to that. I feel like people are looking for my story. I'm never sure. I responded by telling her that I'm twenty-nine and proceeded to turn my attention to Alexa. As time went on, we all chatted, but it really struck me that this is what it means to be in a room full of widows. I don't fit in here.

Thursday, October 10th, 2013 at 9:00 pm
The Dark Place

During my times of infertility and miscarriages, I would call it the dark place. I guess really what I was referring to was depression. That feeling of loss and hurt. I'm there again now. This time for a different reason. I had been doing so well and really nothing has changed. Grief goes in waves and now I'm in the tough part again.

I try to find a reason. Maybe Halloween coming? It was our favorite holiday and the first time we ever hung out. I don't think the cold weather helps either. I cried four times yesterday. Three times were for patients. That's not like me. Today, getting my haircut and nails done felt like a burden instead of something exciting.

Reminders of him are everywhere and I miss him. A new yogurt place opened in the mall. He would have been so excited. I had a different manicurist today who asked if my husband worked too. I didn't know whether to just say I didn't have a husband or tell him he died. Vacation is coming in a few days. I need it. I hate that he won't be there, but I'm determined to have fun.

Tuesday, October 15th, 2013 at 10:08 pm
Vacation

People always say they need a vacation. The problem is that your world is still waiting for you when you come back. My world isn't bad, don't get me wrong, but being in another state doesn't change anything. Alex is still gone and not coming back. I still have milestones to face without him. At night, I'm still alone and lonely.

Nonetheless, it all seems so much easier to face when the ocean is right outside your bedroom door. I have the same responsibilities I usually have. I have work to do. I still have to take care of Alexa, but that doesn't bother me. I would eventually start to miss home, but right now, I'm loving it here and don't want this week to end.

Friday, October 18th, 2013 at 11:06 am
Photography

Since Alex died, I have rarely taken real photos. It has only been when someone has asked me to. I immediately closed the business when he died and sold some of the cameras. I kept his and was not even thinking of bringing it with me on vacation. Then, I was asked to do pregnancy portraits while we were here. I, of course, agreed.

I'm not 100% comfortable doing it on my own. Alex was better. I wasn't finding enjoyment in it without him. Taking out the camera always felt like it was HIS stuff. I took the portraits yesterday, and had fun.

Last night was a full moon. I tried to photograph it, but I didn't bring a tripod. I wasn't nearly as successful as I would like, but enjoyed trying to figure it out. I woke up this morning as the sun started to come up over the water. It's cloudy so I cannot get a true sunrise, but it is still absolutely beautiful. So here I am, out on the deck with our camera equipment, asking Alex to give me some beautiful photos.

Sunday, October 27th, 2013 at 11:25 pm
That's Her...

Sometimes I find myself being self-conscious about my child's behavior. While on vacation, Alexa got sick in a restaurant. Most people understand kids get sick, but do you want to be the person seated near me at that time? I was with a group of people. I cleaned her up and she was fine, but I couldn't help the embarrassment. The table next to us left. There I was, with three couples and my child. Boy, does that scream single mom. Later in the night, an older woman came up to me and told me how I did a great job with her. That was very nice, but felt oh so condescending to be viewed as a young single mom that needs reassurance.

Yesterday, Alexa and I went to a baby shower. Now of course, single or not, this was for women only, so I would be alone regardless. It was a rough day for a toddler, but she did great. She sat in the car for two hours and then was forced to behave at a party all day. She wanted to run around and I had to chase her. I know this is in my head, but I couldn't help but feel that people wondered why she didn't stay home with her dad. Thinking about it more, I wondered how many people knew and were thinking, "That's the girl."

Most people commented that she did well, but one crazy comment out of left field left me speechless. Towards the end of the party when Alexa was getting restless, I walked her back and forth in a stroller. I was stopped by a woman who said, "You remind me of one of those carnival games going back and forth that you need to shoot." What?! I didn't even respond.

Tuesday, October 29th, 2013 at 11:57 pm
Halloween is Approaching

I've been half-dreading and half-looking forward to Halloween. It is my favorite holiday and has a lot of past significance. Seven years ago, Alex and I had just started talking. We hung out for the first time on Halloween night. He admitted later that he basically duped me into a date. We had worked together for months, but had never really spoken until that week. Suddenly the random guy who fixed my computer and got my coffee out of the vending machine when it got stuck was paying attention to me. We communicated on MySpace and emailed back and forth for days.

On Halloween, he mentioned that he would be watching scary movies alone. I (half-jokingly) asked if he wanted to come hand out candy with me. He immediately responded that he would see me later. I went about my day and at 6 pm, the phone rang. He was telling me he was headed to my house. I had no idea he knew where I lived! Thankfully, I gave him the chance to explain that I live in a house that his best friend rented before me.

I remember asking him if he was driving a spaceship. His car was so loud! We spent a few hours awkwardly watching "Dawn of the Dead" while sitting across the room from each other. He left early and gave me an even more awkward hug goodbye. I turned around and went out to a bar with another guy, haha. Somehow in the next few days, we became inseparable and instantly fell madly in love. Cheesy, I know.

Two years ago on Halloween, Alex was away for work and I decided to take a pregnancy test, even though I knew it could be too early to tell. We had been struggling with infertility for so long, I just couldn't wait. It was so faint, I could barely tell it was positive. I have Alexa to prove it was. I have such fond memories of haunted houses and hayrides every year we were together. I can't help but wonder if someone will ever sweep me off my feet like he did. Does it happen more than once?

This year, I have the excitement of taking Alexa trick-or-treating for the first time, and going to her daycare Halloween party. It will be hard without him, but she will make it a happy day.

Today, I decorated his grave for the holiday. I was worried that decorating a grave for Halloween could be considered disrespectful. I mean, it is a holiday of ghosts and goblins and cemeteries. I decided that I didn't care. He deserves decorations for a special day. I'm really trying to get in the spirit of Halloween like I have before.

Thursday, October 31st, 2013 at 12:23 pm
It's Here

The anxiety is getting to me. I'm having a hard time even forcing myself to act normal today. Days with a 31 in them make me feel like crap, and now my favorite holiday does too.

Seven years ago at this time, I had no idea I was about to start dating the man I would marry. Ten months ago at this time, I had no idea I would lose him that night. Fortunately, today is not about me, so I'm going to put on my big girl panties, put this Tinkerbell costume on, and go to Alexa's daycare party. After all, today is for her.

November 2013

Saturday, November 2nd, 2013 at 1:29 am
Not So Desirable

The subject of dating has come up on multiple occasions. What is the right amount of time? In the therapy world, it is suggested that the majority of people are ready by one year. Statistics show that men remarry in only one year, yet women take five years.

As time has passed, I am often asked if I am ready. How do you really know? This subject has been a running joke between some of my friends and family.

Just imagine my online dating profile: "My name is Heather. I'm 4'7, have seven cats, two dogs, and a toddler. I live in the house my husband died in. My child comes first and always will. My husband will always hold a piece of my heart and I will talk about him. Can't handle that? See ya! I smoke and I'm only quitting when I'm ready. I won't move. I won't get rid of my pets. I don't deal with drama or games. I will easily walk away. Have a gun? Not interested. Mental illness? Not doing that again. Looking for someone to have kids with? I physically may not be able to provide that. If that's a deal breaker, move on. I will not share money again. Catch you in a lie and I'm gone. If you don't answer the phone, I will get scared and think you're dead. My child is biracial. Racist? Move on. I will correct your grammar. My life is public. Don't like that? I'm not the one for you."

Doesn't sound too desirable does it? I'm okay with that.

Monday, November 4th, 2013 at 3:09 am
A Penny for Your Thoughts

It wasn't supposed to be this way. I'm not supposed to be alone and lonely after Alexa goes to bed. I'm not supposed to be wondering what the future holds for me. You were my future. I can't believe you are my past. I shouldn't still wake up from nightmares of you. You were supposed to be the happy part of my dreams. I miss your touch. I miss your voice. I can do it without you. I know I'll be fine. I know I'll move on, but I shouldn't have to.

Saturday, November 9th, 2013 at 5:10 am
Hell and Back

I decided I was ready and wanted to try dating. I met someone who gave me butterflies again. Something I never thought I would be able to feel again. I made a conscious effort not to compare things to Alex. I knew that wasn't right. He was understanding about my life and what dating a widow entails. I was amazed at how not-so-awful it was and I could be comfortable with someone else. When he didn't answer me, I panicked and convinced myself he was dead, not considering the logical explanations. Just part of the deal in my crazy screwed up head.

Then came the lying, the drama, and the stress, not what I signed up for. I hate dating. I hate the games. I hate the anxiety of it all. It was never like that with Alex. Here I go comparing. So yeah, this sucks. I've been through hell and back. This is nothing. Life on my own is better. I don't think I can handle a relationship. It was a step towards moving on and I'm thankful I tried.

Tuesday, November 12th, 2013 at 12:42 pm
Someone to Talk to

I met someone yesterday who recently lost a family member. She repeatedly mentioned it and described it as a tragedy, sudden, and unexpected. It was almost as if she was trying to get me to ask how, but I won't ask. A death is sad regardless, and it doesn't really matter how it happened. Finally, she blurted out (without my asking), "He shot himself," and proceeded to act as if she needed to explain every detail of what the family was dealing with.

I'm sure she was looking to get it off her chest, but I need to be professional and take care of her dog, not reminisce about more memories I do not want. At that point, I stated, "My husband did the same thing. I know there is a lot of stress right now." Of course, I got the pity face, as I usually do. I then moved the conversation back to the situation at hand.

At the end of the visit, she started telling me everything. It was then that I realized she really just needed someone to talk to and I've been there. I listened and gave small tokens of reassurance and she was so grateful. Again, my tragic experience helped someone with theirs. It didn't matter how upsetting the conversation was to me. I made her feel just a little bit better.

Sunday, November 17th, 2013 at 3:50 pm
Under the Weight of Life, Things Seem Brighter on the Other Side

Music has always been something that can really touch me. Alex and I disagreed about the important part of a song. He always felt that the melody was all that mattered, while I argued that it was the lyrics. Lyrics touch me more now than ever. It seems like the times that I cry now are usually unexpectedly from songs. Months back, a good friend told me to listen to this song. I heard it again recently. She said it reminded her of Alex. When I first started listening, I was horrified.

"Story of a man,
Who decided not to breathe
Turned red, purple, then blue.
Colorful indeed
No matter how his friends begged,
Well, he would not concede,
And now he's dead."

I did not go any further and questioned why she would send this to me. Her response was that she hadn't even realized what the other lyrics were, except this:

"But, oh God, Under the weight of life, Things seem brighter on the other side…"

Now I get it. I still think this is a terrible song. And I certainly did not need the visual from the first line, but it's true. Under the weight of life, things can seem brighter on the other side.

Tuesday, November 19th, 2013 at 10:25 pm
The Elephant in the Room

For the majority of grievers, this time of year brings about the undeniable "elephant in the room." The holidays are coming and reminders are everywhere. Halloween hadn't even gotten here yet, but Christmas music was already playing in the mall and Christmas trees were going up in stores.

Facing one day is difficult enough, but you face the holidays every day from October to January. What is the proper etiquette? Do you acknowledge the holidays and ignore that they bother you? Do you hide? For me, I have decided to go with a happy medium. Thanksgiving is not an issue, as I usually work and will this year too. Then comes the rest.

Originally, I discussed boycotting Christmas. However, it would be harder to spend the day trying to ignore what it is, rather than just sucking it up and dealing with it. Not only is it a major family holiday without him, last Christmas was the last week I had with him. In my situation, I have a child, and though she really is not old enough to understand, I want to attempt to enjoy her second Christmas.

We went to see Santa already. That did not go so well, but worked out somewhat in the end. I do not ever put up a tree, as it just does not mesh well with seven cats, so nothing will change there. Part of me says I will put up stockings. The other part says I don't want to see just two. With everyone talking about Christmas shopping, I am saddened that I won't have that special someone to shop for. I already found so many things he would like. Why did I used to think he was difficult to buy for?

I can say it's just a day, but it is really an entire season to deal with. After that comes New Year's Eve. My one year "sadiversary." Thankfully, I will be escaping to the beautiful Outer Banks for the week, but still, that's just geography. Not only will I have no one to kiss at midnight, I fear reliving the feelings of one year earlier. As usual, I'll get through it. I always do, but I am looking forward to the arrival of spring!

Saturday, November 23rd, 2013 at 2:04 pm
They're Reading My Life

"It was December 31, 2012 and Heather's husband had suddenly taken his own life. Her life drastically changed, in that one short moment, forever. On Thursday, January 24, 2013, Heather created a blog. She needed to heal and also wanted to help others navigate through the grieving process. 'My name is Heather and this is a journal of my life after losing the love of my life to mental illness and suicide. My hope is to help others out there who may be travelling a similar path as I am.' Right away, she decided that this experience and major life change would not kill her and it hasn't! Heather is determined to create something positive from a terrible, preventable tragedy in her life, and the lives of others affected. Since she was unable to save him, she hopes to save another life, and prevent someone from the heartache she has experienced. She is working hard to help end the silence about mental illness and suicide, and has become certified in grief recovery. Heather has donated to and participated in multiple fundraisers for suicide prevention and other organizations. Not only is she rising above her grief and building a new life for her and her young daughter, she is determined to help anyone she can along the way."

I stood at the entrance to the stage, listening to these words and almost could not even breathe. It was me they were describing to a room full of people. My trauma was being exposed over the loudspeaker to a bunch of unsuspecting strangers. I write about my life for the world to see, but here I was, vulnerable and being stared at as everyone heard these words. What were people thinking? I made it across the stage without tripping and with a few breaths involved. I was so surprised at how uneasy I was literally putting a face to my story.

Later in the evening, I began to dig through the gifts accompanied by the award. Free gun classes at Shooters Choice (the gun range of Alex's choice). All I could think was, "Gee, the irony is not lost on me." I was more bothered by two tickets to the Harrington Casino Buffet. Boy, did he love that place. I kept thinking, who will I go with now?

It was a nice night with family and friends. I'm still amazed that I was considered a "DelMarvalous Woman."

Saturday, November 30th, 2013 at 3:47 pm
Love

Yesterday, I found myself in a conversation about the difference between loving someone and being in love with them. I was told that I am no longer in love with Alex. At first, I wasn't sure how I felt about that statement, but quickly came to the realization that it is true. After eleven months without any tangible relationship with him, how could I be? I can't see him, hear him, feel him, etc. He's gone. Eventually that love needs to change, and it has. I love the memories and I love the person he was, but he's just a memory now.

Seems strange to think that I have been in love with someone since I was twenty-two, and now at twenty-nine, the feeling is gone. If this never changed, no one would ever move on. Though this change in feelings was clearly not a conscious decision, the realization feels pretty good and pretty terrible at the same time. I will always love him, but someday maybe I will be in love again.

◆◆◆

December 2013

Wednesday, December 4th, 2013 at 1:27 am
Just Some Random Thoughts Tonight

To the TV show "Dads" – joking about suicide and calling it "the easy way out" is not funny and very disrespectful.

I hate being sick and not having Alex here to take care of me.

I loved having Santa come by on the fire truck for Alexa, but for me, I didn't like the sirens and flashing lights in front of my house. I was able to hold back the tears and smile for Alexa.

I hate that last year Alex was outside with us to see Santa.

I hate that I take Alexa to check-ups and she doesn't have a dad with her. I can't text him about it either.

I'm going through the motions of Christmas. I can't hide from it. I think I'm looking forward to doing some baking. Okay, it's not baking, it's Oreo ball-making.

I love Oreo balls, but it reminds me of the funeral because that night was the first time I had them.

I hate the winter. I really do. I have no desire for snow. I hate being cold. I'll be a happier person in the spring.

I have let go of my anger. I still truly believe that he didn't do this and "mind monsters" did, but I still can't help but wonder how you can leave a baby behind and do it on a holiday.

It bothers me that the guy on "Jeopardy" tonight looks like Alex.

I miss everything about being married. I miss having another half. I miss having someone to talk to. I miss the sweet text messages. I miss sleeping next to someone. I miss having someone to run to with any thought I have. I miss being a family. I miss date nights. I miss fighting and making up. I miss the way he looked at me.

Tuesday, December 10th, 2013 at 10:22 pm
Wake Me Up When December Ends

December brings a lot of ups and downs. I've mentioned before that I don't like the cold and how it gets dark so early. I'm not sure I ever realized how much I hate it. Motivation is low and I just don't have the energy I normally do. I'm spending more time sleeping than ever. I have been sick and my headaches have been rough, so I guess that makes sense anyway.

Every day, I look at the date and wonder what was going on on this date last year. I had no idea how my world was about to change. What was going on in his head that I was missing? What should I have been doing differently? Were we going through a winter depression?

The holidays are hard and compounded by the idea that the one year is creeping up on me. What will it feel like to get past that dreadful date? Will I feel relief? Will I relive last year? I really can't say. I am trying to get through everything associated with Christmas. I'm trying to get excited for Alexa. I don't think I have it in me to send Christmas cards and I haven't been able to put up our stockings. I'm struggling with the idea that he won't come home with a cute Christmas gift that he can't wait until Christmas to give me.

Though I hate the snow, I'm looking forward to taking Alexa sledding for the first time. I'm crazy excited for my next tattoo appointment. It's just the therapy I need. I'm half-looking forward to vacation. I want to go, but I know that dreadful date will arrive when I am there. And still, I will have no one to kiss at midnight like I had for six New Years'. That is if I'm awake anyway. Clearly last year, that was the last thing on my mind on that date. I'm excited for the next two weekends with my friends who are not going to leave me to be alone on some rough weekends. Still, I'm looking forward to spring.

Tuesday, December 17th, 2013 at 3:39 pm
Insert Cranky Title Here

Lately, I feel like I'm back at the beginning of all this. I'm replaying that night, trying to change what I said, and fix the outcome. I'm wondering again at what point in time would I choose to go back and try to change things. I'm pondering the different outcomes. I'm replaying my life with him. I thought I was past all of this. Apparently, it comes back.

Seeing Christmas lights while driving home at night bothers me. It reminds me of the days right after his death. Everyone's Christmas lights were still up, and here they are again. The random things that become reminders are strange. Again, I sit here shocked that there's no way out of this, no way to fix it. I'm baffled that an amazing man chose to leave this world at twenty-nine years old. I should have had so much more time with him. I'm annoyed that there will never be anyone like him.

In talking to other people, I totally get that in that moment, nothing matters. You can't see the negative impact on those around you. I know he thought this was better for me. I can tell myself that all I want, but still, this isn't better.

I thought I reached acceptance. I'm not a fan of the whole, "Why me?" Bad things happen to good people. Bad things happen to everyone. Really though, why did this happen to me? Why did this happen to Alexa? Right now, all I can see is that the holidays are coming and I'm alone. The man that promised me forever is gone. I'm back to one day at a time. "Just keep swimming" and get through another day. That's all I can do.

Wednesday, December 25th, 2013 at 11:28 pm
Christmas

I made it through Christmas. This month has been hard. There's no denying that. This week has been the hardest. There were days that I just couldn't force being normal. The smile on my face was fake and the tears were right there and ready at every minute of the day. I lost all motivation and had times where I couldn't force myself to do anything.

I'm constantly told how strong I am, yet no one truly knows what goes on in my head. I don't always feel so strong. Friends visited the last two weekends and kept me going. Work forced me to keep moving. The toddler yelling down the hall forced me out of bed each day.

As usual, the days leading up to a holiday are worse than the actual holiday. I cried so many times on Monday and I don't even know why. Christmas music was my arch enemy as if mocking me, trying to bring out the tears. Then, the days arrived.

I brought Alexa to visit Alex yesterday and put flowers on his grave. I asked her if she wanted to go and she said, "Yes." Though when I asked her if she knew what I meant, she said, "No." I know she doesn't quite get it but feel that if she visits now, it will always be normal to her. I know I have a lot of major explaining to do someday (and I'm dreading it even now). I hope that the more we visit, the more comfortable she will be with it. Who knows? I really have no experience on this. I'm just figuring it out as I go along. I guess that's how motherhood is anyway.

I cooked Christmas Eve dinner and was excited to make it an all crock pot meal, using three of them. I love crock pots. I was just discussing getting a fifth one. Technically seventh because I have two mini ones. Slightly obsessed...

Dinner turned out great. The night wasn't so bad. I expected today to be awful. I shouldn't expect the worst, but I do in this case. I took photos with Alexa and watched her open gifts. Recently, someone said that they thought that Christmas was the best when they were a kid, but it's really the best when you have a kid. It was great that Alexa could understand and open gifts herself this year.

Of course, last year, Alex was still here. I had six more days with him. I wish I had known. In six days, I will have survived a year. I can't believe it's only six more days. Part of me feels like it took forever to get here and the other part of me feels like it can't have been that long. 359 days since I saw him, kissed him, touched him. How is that possible?

Saturday, I am leaving for vacation. I started packing today.

I hope I can enjoy it as a vacation and not be caught up in the date. We'll see. Will New Year's Eve ever be okay? Will Christmas ever be fully happy again? Last year, we took a photo as a family. This year, I took a photo as a single mom. I was still so excited for the experience with Alexa. Being a mom is amazing, even if it is not the experience I pictured. I miss you, Mow. Merry Christmas.

January 2014

Wednesday, January 1st, 2014 at 1:06 pm
A New Year

This year already started out better than the last. Last year, I woke up to the realization that this wasn't a nightmare. My life had actually become a nightmare. This year, I woke up to sounds of Alexa and the ocean outside.

I made it through the one year yesterday. Honestly, it wasn't as bad as I had expected. However, I'm glad it's over.

We ate, drank, toasted him, walked on the beach, and did some outlet shopping. I had some tough moments and paced the entire kitchen and top floor for the time when it was happening one year ago.

At night, the bar across the street had a New Year's Eve 5K. I ended up choosing to do the one-mile walk instead of the 5K run, but couldn't help picturing Alex running ahead in his toe shoes.

Thank you for everyone who checked in on me and has been there for me this past year. I can't tell you what it means to me. It truly has been the worst year of my life, yet I have had some of the most incredible moments with Alexa this year. Here's to another year of new milestones and experiences with my princess and lifesaver. Maybe next New Year's Eve will be a little better.

Thursday, January 2nd, 2014 at 1:11 pm
2014

It's January. I couldn't wait for December to end and to finally get past the huge one year milestone. The truth is, today and yesterday felt like any other day. Nothing changed. I did not have any huge revelations. My world did not have any excessive changes. It's just another day. I did not make any resolutions. I don't need to.

I've made the promises to myself to continue being the best mom that I can be, take better care of myself, keep striving to make a difference, and continue on. I'm still on vacation and feeling pretty good here. I know my normal world is waiting for me at home, and that's okay. There will always be more things to look forward to. The same statement goes when it comes to hard moments ahead. They will always be there.

Monday, January 6th, 2014 at 12:13 am
The Day it Became Real

Tonight, one year ago, was the private viewing for Alex's funeral. So, today is already a much better day than it was one year ago. I survived that week of death, the funeral, and starting a new life. It's not easy, but I'm doing it, and I even find myself happy sometimes.

Despite everything, I felt pretty good today. Vacation is over and my reality is back. I went to his grave in the snow yesterday. I can't believe I've been visiting there for a year. I still miss him every day. I don't know if that ever changes.

I'm starting to notice little things in Alexa's personality that are clearly him. She was referred to as "daddy's little girl" recently. She is. I wish he were here to see it. Tomorrow, I will be working. My first day back after vacation, but it will distract me from what was going on last year. As usual, I will get through it. I always do.

Tuesday, January 7th, 2014 at 2:36 pm
When the Music's Over

For the last week, I keep reflecting on this time last year. I originally feared that I would be reliving last year and it would be incredibly painful. It hasn't been. Each day, I have reminded myself how much better this day is, compared to last year.

When I was aggravated by the rain and traffic yesterday,

I thought back to what I was doing last year. I'll take the traffic any day. I feel good knowing the progress I've made. Today, last year, was ultimately the first day of my new life. The funeral was over and the crowd was leaving. There was no more planning and no more getting things done before the funeral. It was now my real life. It was scary looking at what was ahead. One step at a time, I created my new world. There are no more real changes and no more firsts after yesterday. I've gotten through the first anniversary of everything and every first holiday. We will see what the second year brings.

For the first few weeks, my phone was nuts. If I decided to take a nap, I woke to many texts, Facebook notifications, IMs, missed calls, you name it. Anyone and everyone was contacting me constantly. Plus, the close ones would get scared when I didn't answer. I couldn't keep up, yet it was nice to have constant interaction.

All of this communication has dwindled now. Of course, that is to be expected. People move on with their lives. I still find myself craving constant interaction and still have a lot of friends to consistently chat with. My phone is my lifeline. I've always been very social, but still. I got used to six years of having someone to text and email all day every day.

Thursday, January 30th, 2014 at 3:20 am
"Our Place"

A few months back, I won a dinner for two to a buffet Alex loved. One of my favorite photos of him was taken there. We had not been there in a long time, but I related to it as his place. I refused to waste the tickets. It was a good night with a good friend but still felt strange. I did not like seeing where that photo was taken. I did not like looking through the buffet at all the foods Alex loved. I got through it, like I do everything else.

Recently, I experienced another place that I previously considered as our place. I have vivid memories of going there while Alexa was still in the hospital. We loved unlimited wings night. Alex spent a lot of time there for staff meetings and I would meet him afterwards. This time, however, there was nothing strange. It didn't feel like our place anymore. It was a good experience. I even ate the wings and laughed about some of the memories there.

More steps forward? Who knows? Either way, I'm glad it didn't bother me.

February 2014

Saturday, February 15th, 2014 at 2:28 pm
It's Valentine's Day Again

This year, I decided to completely get through the holiday before writing about it. I started out last year saying that it didn't mean anything, then ate my words. Valentine's Day is all about how you look at it. An anti-single day for couples only? A Hallmark holiday? A day to appreciate your loved ones?

Single or not, it is important to appreciate the people in your life every day. Tell your significant other how much they mean to you. Hug your children whenever you can. Don't wait until the calendar says so or until it's too late. Appreciate the good in yourself every day. Flowers and candy are great (I am a girl), but it's the thought that counts.

Appreciate everyone in your life on a day about love. Thank your best friend, your child, your parents, and the guy who makes you smile even though he's not yours. If you are feeling sad and single, that's okay. There's always next year.

Happy belated Valentine's Day to everyone in my life and to my angel on the other side!

Tuesday, February 25th, 2014 at 7:31 pm
Disney and More

Everyone has been asking me how our trip to Disney was. I could lie and say it's the best place on earth and I can't wait to go back, but I won't. The truth is, it was tough. First, the simple fact is, traveling on a plane alone with a twenty-one-month-old is not easy. I couldn't explain it all to her and had to take things as they come. The multiple people asking if I was traveling alone with her started to get to me. I smiled and said, "Yes," and moved along, but it really bugged me. Yes, I'm alone with her. That's my life. She vomited all over the plane, something I should have expected, and I got through it. Otherwise, she did very well. I was out of my comfort zone. Even though that didn't used to bother me, it does now.

We got through the first day at Magic Kingdom, and though she was really too young to understand it, we had some fun. At the end of the day, upon the realization that I spent a day at Disney without Alex, I cried through the whole monorail ride. She had her first Disney experience without her dad. The last time I was there was with him.

I spent four days with Alex's family, a constant reminder that he should be there with us! This was another experience that reminded me that everything in her life will be experienced without her dad. Overall, anxiety was high. It was a rough experience for her, but we did it. I am at my highest stress levels when I worry about things being tough on her.

I'm moving on and doing well without him. There comes

a point where you have to get past all the trauma and enjoy your life. I'm getting there. Now, my sadness comes from what Alexa misses out on. I'm perfectly capable of raising her on my own, but she shouldn't have to miss out on experiences with her father. It hurts me that she does.

I was discussing parenting with someone recently and said that I figure it out as I go along and don't always know if I'm doing the right thing. The response was, "You won't mess her up." All I could think was that I'm scared I will when I have to tell her the truth. I guess I'll always be scared of that. She didn't deserve this, and neither did I. Those are the cards we were dealt and I will deal with the responsibility of explaining things to her. It sucks that she won't remember him, but as terrible as it sounds, it's better that way. She won't know to miss him.

I see traits in my personality that were not there before. I've never been so insecure and indecisive. Yet, I don't think I've ever been as strong. In the past, I felt my life was set. I had everything I wanted: my job, house, child, and husband. Now, I feel like I don't know where my life is going.

I want my life to be set again. I want to be as happy as I was again. I'll get there I guess. I need to relax and enjoy the ride. I've learned so much about appreciating what you have. I never thought he would be gone. I never thought I wouldn't have the chance to tell him how much he meant to me. I've learned to say what I'm thinking and appreciate every moment. Don't take anyone for granted. I won't ever do that again.

March 2014

Tuesday, March 11th, 2014 at 2:31 am
Time Flies? Or Does It?

Sometimes, it truly amazes me how much time has passed and how different life is now. Other times, I can't believe how relevant he still is in my life and how many things I still relate to him. He still comes up in conversation constantly. He's a huge part of my life and always will be.

I went to the graveyard yesterday and seeing the "2012" on the stone amazed me, considering the fact that it's now 2014. Although, it was still 2012 for only a few hours when he died. I don't go to the graveyard as much and I don't spend as much time as I used to. Part of me feels a little guilty, but that's a normal thing over time.

The photos of him on the wall now feel strange. I can't really put into words why. I don't really want to stare at my past I guess. They are still there and I don't know that I'm in any rush to remove them, but they just don't have the same feeling. Alexa changes every day and I hate that she doesn't have her dad. That little girl has so many people who love her. No matter what I have been through, I will never regret one moment because Alex gave me the most important thing in the world, my baby girl. Well, I guess she isn't really a baby anymore. I'll admit, in the tough moments with her, I beg him for help because he should be here to experience this with me. He's not, and that's okay. It has to be.

It's not a secret to those in my life that I am moving on and dating again. I know Alex would want me to be happy. It sounds cliché, but he wanted the best for me. He just had a strange view of it.

I'm ready and I'm excited to see what the future will bring. It's funny how in the beginning you just can't imagine that it's possible to get to this place, but you really do get there. It's a long, tough, and awful road. You never really get over it, but you get through it. I vowed not to die with him. I haven't and I'm happy with who I've become and the progress I've made. I know he's cheering me on from the other side. I deserve the chance to be happy again.

♦♦♦

April 2014

Tuesday, April 1st, 2014 at 7:59 pm
The Basement

As you are all probably well aware, Alex died in my basement and I still live in that house. I don't spend much time down there, not because I'm scared or anything, but for the sheer fact that it's become a mess of a catch-all for anything I don't have space for. I've been talking about cleaning it out for ages.

Today, a Fios installation technician had to go in the basement to set up my new internet. Upon looking at the way Alex had the routers and everything set up, he exclaimed, "Holy shiiiii...!" Later, I overheard him on the phone telling his boss that my basement set-up looked like Microsoft. The genius in Alex made it horribly complicated to get new internet service, as they couldn't figure out how to bypass what he had done. I was getting frustrated fast.

Meanwhile, looking around, I decided today was the day. I spent four hours cleaning, packing, going through stuff, and throwing things away. I ran up and down the stairs with heavy items probably a hundred times. I found bags and bags of garbage left down there from the last time he cleaned down there. I went through and threw out the most random things of his. I deflated the Slip 'N Slide from his birthday party. Laying on the floor while it was deflating, I couldn't help but notice I was laying right near the spot I found him in. I could even still see flakes of blood rolling around on the floor. I just laughed it off. I guess that's where I'm at now.

I obviously had to explain to the Verizon technician that it was Alex who had installed everything downstairs and why I didn't know how to change passwords, etc. In talking about the setup, he said, "Well he thought he was doing the right thing at the time." Funny how close that comment hit home. He thought that about other things, too. Alex was probably laughing from the other side. I'm glad I FINALLY cleaned out the basement!

Friday, April 4th, 2014 at 1:05 pm
I'll Never be Normal

I'm learning that no matter how much time has passed and life has moved on, I will never be completely okay. I'll never be normal again or the person I once was. Things in movies bother me every time. Almost every movie mentions or jokes about suicide. So many movies have guns in them. I've been doing very well at laughing it off.

One of my major coping mechanisms is to make inappropriate jokes about the situation to get me through. Last night was different. The sight of someone getting shot in the head and laying there dead sent me into a panic. I jumped up, couldn't breathe, and felt like vomiting. I tried to calm down and ended bursting into tears. Here's the kicker: I sobbed about my husband on my boyfriend's chest. Even typing that sounds strange. All I can really say is, that's my life.

Sunday, April 13th, 2014 at 11:26 am
"Thirty, Flirty, and Thriving..."

"Why the thirties are the best years of your life." This is a quote from one of my favorite movies. I will get back to that.

Yesterday, one year ago, I turned twenty-nine. Alex was gone for a short three months and I was still in the dark place. I had to work that day, but in the morning, I called my mom to say that I literally couldn't move. It was my birthday and I was without him. The pain was unbearable and I just couldn't pick myself up. I made it through the day and chalked it up to surviving another first. What was the last year of my twenties to bring? This past year has brought about a lot of firsts, a lot of changes, and both pain and happiness. I made it.

Yesterday, I celebrated with my amazing friends, awesome family, and wonderful boyfriend. It was truly a great day. Alex was surely there in spirit and in stories. I think he would be so proud of the woman I have become and happy to see my new life.

I've been thinking about this quote, "Thirties are the best year of your life," and have been bothered thinking that life could ever be better after his death. I'm happy again and excited to see what this next years have to bring.

What does it feel like to be thirty? Well today, my whole body hurts.

Monday, April 21st, 2014 at 7:24 pm
Easter #2

Another second holiday has passed and it was good. I've written before about how life moves forward. I usually work on

Easter and last year, basically avoided the whole holiday. This year, I went back to making eggs, Easter bread, and cookies. We were unsuccessful at getting Alexa to sit with the Easter bunny, but she still got all dressed up and tried. I had a small Easter celebration at my house and had a first holiday experience with my new guy and his family. Alexa was excited about her Easter basket, even though she can't totally understand yet. I visited Alex this week and brought him some Easter flowers. I still think he probably thinks it is stupid to waste money on flowers, but I do it anyway.

This holiday was happy, and I wasn't just trying to make it through. I'm not saying I did it this time. I'm saying it was a good weekend. Amazing how things change. My little girl is growing up fast. I will always be disappointed she doesn't have her father to experience all of this with her, but I know he is watching her from the other side. She has so many people that love her and though no one will ever replace him, I am happy to see her build a bond with someone else in my life. As I have always said, we truly are a package deal.

Last year, I wrote how saddened I was watching my dad take apart the swing set I purchased for her. That was something I felt Alex should have been a part of. Spring is here and over the past few weekends, we have started to rebuild it in my yard. When I say "we," I mean "they," as I don't really do any of the work. I'm thankful that I have my dad, my cousin, and my boyfriend ready and willing to do this for her.

I've also written in the past about a song lyric that says, "We're not broken just bent and can learn to love again." I wrote that I was pretty sure I was broken. Though at the time it certainly felt like it, I had different thoughts when I heard the song again. I really can love again. Things are very different now and everything feels different. I feel bad saying I'm happy again, but I am. It feels good to not just be existing anymore. However, I still miss him every day and I always will, but maybe just in a different way now.

Sunday, April 27th, 2014 at 3:52 am
Worst Days

Do you ever think about what the worst days of your life are? For the sake of consistency and mental clarity, focus on your adult life. I should really say that the worst day was the day Alex died, but was it? That day is a blur. I can honestly say, after finding him, I was no longer mentally able to grasp the concept of what happened. I couldn't feel anything. I couldn't understand anything. The days and weeks surrounding it were the overall worst.

Today was a horrible day. I watched one of the closest people in the world to me have to say goodbye to her mother. I have no idea what this feels like. I know that watching her heartache and agony was so incredibly awful. I wanted so badly to take her pain away, but I can't. I could only hold her hand (and hair back) and tell her that this sucks and it's not fair, but she will survive.

It was a long day. I left at 5 am (two hour drive) to spend the morning with her, go to the service and dinner, and hold her hand through the emotional experience of when it becomes real. I may not have lost a parent, but I certainly understand when it becomes real. I have vivid memories of watching another close friend say goodbye to her father. I knew that was one of the worst moments of my life, just watching the sheer agony on her face. I knew I would face that again today.

Three women, friends for many years, and we now have all held each other's hands through such experiences. I can think of so many things that best friends are for. This may be the worst thing to experience with a best friend, but it may be the most important.

Next comes the man who lost his wife. The situations are certainly different and I cannot say I know how he feels, but I know the path. I know how hard tomorrow will be when he wakes up and everything is over. Everyone is gone and his new life will begin. I don't wish that upon anyone. In talking with him, his tear-filled eyes looked at me as someone who has done this before (which felt so strange). The only advice I could offer was to take it one day at a time, one step each day. There really is nothing I can say or do to take away this man's pain. I've spent the past week thinking about where was I the next day, the third day, and so on.

Today was as emotional as any funeral is. I was thankful to be given the important task of babysitter. I got to focus on the needs of this child (about the same age as mine) and attempt to ignore that the sheer idea of what was going on around me, which brought back horrible memories. As people had asked, I did relive some things today, but it was not about me and I certainly was not going to let it be.

I spent every minute with my friend that I could, but had to get back to being a mom. I was so drained and migraine-ridden that I couldn't wait for the day to be over. I know that Alex was there with me, helping our friend in her time of need.

May 2014

Monday, May 5th, 2014 at 4:18 pm
The Things That May Brings

I've written previously about how some days are covered in reminders. Out of nowhere, a day that should seem rather normal just screams Alex everywhere. Seeing a car like his STILL stops me mid-sentence. Though at times now, it does just make me smile.

Songs still can have a very positive or negative effect on me. Yesterday was one of those days. I started to wonder if he was trying to tell me something. What was the significance of that day? It didn't get me down, but it did have my mind wandering a bit too much. Thanks to Facebook, I realized that six years ago yesterday was my bachelorette party. Could that be it? I'll never know for sure, but was my subconscious thinking about it?

Based on that fact, I thought about our wedding anniversary coming up. How is that supposed to feel now? Just another day? Will it be sad? I don't really know. I'm starting to wonder how I should handle that day. I'm guessing it would be a good day for a distraction. Maybe I should make it a happy day and don't give my mind time to run amok by sitting at home. I guess all I can say right now is we'll see what happens.

Alexa's birthday is coming up soon. Though it was hard to get through it last year, I'm confident this year will be better. It hurts to look back on how little she was when he died, versus the child she is now. He has missed so much of her life! Still, I'm so proud of her and will never be able to put into words how amazing it is to be a mom, even with everything we have already been through in her short life.

Wednesday, May 14th, 2014 at 7:48 pm
Mother's Day

Here we are. Another second holiday come and gone. I can honestly say that this was my first good Mother's Day. Last year, I was still messed up. Things were still so hard and miserable. I wanted so badly to enjoy my first Mother's Day, but I really couldn't. I was so upset that I did not have Alex to share it with that nothing else mattered to me.

My daughter does not have a father to help her with a gift for me. I debated buying myself something, but I didn't. Understand that I am not looking at this in a materialistic sense. However, some small recognition is always nice. Though it is the best thing that ever happened to me, being a mom is tough, and (I believe) being a single mom is tougher.

Two years ago, I was very pregnant and spent the night in the hospital after having a random seizure. This is not how I wished to spend the holiday either. When it came to multiple years prior, I was struggling with infertility and this holiday was a day to remind me that I was not a mom. Mother's Day always seemed to be a dark day for me.

This year was happy. I am mentally in a different place and am able to enjoy life most of the time. It was a quiet day spent with family and involved a lot of food. I was excited to spend time with my little girl and paint her nails for the first time! I got a very sweet gift, of which I was not expecting. Nothing major, but major thought was put into it and it made me very happy.

As I mentioned earlier, May brings a lot of very happy events that ultimately bring significant sadness with them. Mother's Day turned out very well. I have a lot of hope for Alexa's birthday being great. I am sure, somehow, I will get through our wedding anniversary again. Maybe it won't be so bad, maybe.

Thursday, May 15th, 2014 at 3:57 pm
Spiritual, Not Religious

What happens when you die? Clearly, no one really knows for sure. Everyone has different beliefs, and those beliefs build the foundation of our grief or even our peace with the loss. I try not to push too far when I discuss what my beliefs are, though I have alluded to them in this blog before. I believe everyone has the right to their own opinion. What I believe works for me.

So here are some thoughts:

I routinely refer to the process after death as crossing over. I do not make the determination between heaven, hell, or anything in between. To me, this means crossing over to the spirit world. I have mentioned before that I believe spirits walk among us. I believe they can visit as they wish and can take any form necessary to spark our interest. I believe spirits do not cross over right away and can linger until the time is right.

When it came to Alex, I used to feel he was always with me. I couldn't see him, but I knew he was there. Just a feeling, I guess. When I needed proof and asked, he would provide it. Though I never actually saw or heard him. I believe that spirits are able to come through in dreams and I can clearly tell the difference between a dream and a visit. I only have recollection of one dream which was real. I believe, given the circumstances, Alex was unable to cross over until I was okay on my own. I am now and I believe he has left. This is not to say he cannot check in as needed and visit Alexa, but I no longer need him constantly. As far as I am concerned, he is always welcome to visit her and I hope he does often.

I have been asked before why I don't write about God. Yes, I do believe in a God. However I don't believe that God has protected me, saved me, or got me through this. I did the work. I grieved and WORKED through this. If He is protecting me, why didn't He protect Alex? He was a good person and he was sick, but what's meant to be will be. Although he chose to end his life prematurely, I still believe that somehow, it must have been his time. I know that it is out of my control and I may never fully understand why or the depth behind everything that happened. The same goes for someone who died of natural causes. We will never truly know why it was their time.

I do not have a formal religion and do not feel I need one. Nothing against those that do, whatever works for you. When it comes to Alexa, Alex was wholeheartedly against raising her with a formal religion and I will continue to raise her with that agreement. Furthermore, I will not raise her in any religion that will teach her that her father went to hell for a mistake he made. Again, I believe Alex was a good man and I do not think a God would turn his back on him, as many religions teach.

Though not a formal religion, I am a minister of the Universal Life Church. What does this mean? Basically, I went online and got ordained to have the ability to perform weddings. I am excited to be marrying my first couple next month. Just as exciting is the idea that this organization promotes equality of all religions and beliefs. We all have a right to what we believe in and to not be judged for it. Everyone is different, no better, no worse, and should all be respected.

Do we really need someone to tell us to help others, be a good person, and have appropriate morals? I don't think so.

Wednesday, May 28th, 2014 at 7:19 pm
Happy Birthday, Alexa!

It certainly has been a crazy week. My little princess turned two! It is so interesting how I look at all of this now. So many people say to me that time flies, but does it? Part of me cannot believe that my little girl is two. She is not a baby anymore! However, looking back on everything we have been through since she has been born puts it into a whole different perspective. It feels like ages ago that Alex was alive. I really feel like it was a lifetime ago, and I haven't seen him in forever. Seven months. She was only seven months old when he passed away and now she is two!

A completely different child and a completely different life.

It was a big birthday party weekend. On Thursday, I rushed around doing a million things to get ready. On Friday, Alexa's grandparents came to visit. This is always a rough experience for me, as it is a huge reminder that Alex is gone. I always end up in tears discussing him, rehashing what happened, and looking at the people who raised him. I am so thankful that they want a relationship with their granddaughter, but it will always be a source of anxiety for me. Just as I can't, they will never truly be able to understand what happened and I will never be able to give them the answers they deserve. I try, but I just don't have them.

I tried very hard to enjoy my daughter's birthday, but there was just so much pain surrounding it. I thought so much about the day she was born and the scary but incredible experience Alex and I shared that day. Next thing I knew, Friday was over and it was time to party!

It was an amazing day. Alexa and I had so much fun with friends and family. With the bouncy house, I got to act like a kid again and yet a parent at the same time. I am so thankful for everyone that came to celebrate her. She is loved by so many.

In the aftermath, I am sore and tired. Too much fun, but also a lot of work cleaning, cooking, and hosting. I cannot believe it is over! Before I know it, I will be planning birthday number three.

I knew it may be hard. I knew some tears may be shed. I knew there would be fun. It was overall a great experience. I know Alex was there in spirit and I feel great watching Alexa grow up in my new world. I'm doing the best that I can as a mom. That's all I can ask for.

There is still one more May event to get through, our anniversary. On Saturday, we would have been married for six years. I know this may be difficult, but I am going into it hoping to cherish the memories and move on with the day. No matter what happened, it was still one of the best days of my life.

June 2014

Thursday, June 5th, 2014 at 3:14 pm
Life Moves Pretty Fast

It has been a busy few weeks! Aren't I always saying that lately?

The biggest overall thing that has happened is that after almost a year and a half, I sold Alex's bicycle. I toyed with the idea numerous times, but really didn't put full effort into it. I knew it would be incredibly difficult to part with, but what good was it doing just sitting in my garage? It was taking up space and, more importantly, going to waste.

I won't say it was the easiest thing on earth to say goodbye to. It wasn't, but it was the right thing to do. It was his pride and joy and really meant the world to him. I'm glad someone can appreciate it and get use out of it. It certainly feels weird to see the empty spot in the garage where it used to hang. Still, it did not feel as awful as I expected. Honestly, that's usually the case with these things. The anticipation tends to be so much harder than the actual event.

Next up is our wedding anniversary. I planned a beach day, as to not sit home and think about it. I know my idle mind creates terrible scenarios. I tried to make it as normal of a day as possible and it really was. I watched our wedding recap video and smiled with tears in my eyes. You really can laugh and cry at the same time. It was so much easier to get through this year than last. More often than not, I look back with happy memories. No matter what happened, it was an amazing day and I will never regret it. I liked being married. Although we did not live happily ever after, as the video says, I have wonderful memories to hang onto.

This week, two years ago, Alexa was still in the hospital. I look back to each day, thinking of what we were doing at this point. It was amazing, scary, stressful, and beautiful. I'm so glad we shared that experience and of course, so thankful that she is a happy healthy girl after all of that.

I've learned to take advantage of each day, live life to the fullest, and be as happy as I can be. I guess a huge life-changing experience will do that. The term "life is short" never meant so much to me.

Wednesday, June 18th, 2014 at 4:14 pm
Father's Day

Father's Day has come and gone. I am finally taking the time to write about it. There are a lot of mixed feelings and emotions here! First, Alexa is not old enough to understand what Father's Day is or even what a father is at this point. I'm thankful for this, yet I know it will change in years to come. It's just another one of those things that I will figure out as I go along.

Earlier in the week, I was pulled aside at daycare to discuss their Father's Day project. It was brought to the attention of the teacher that the activity she picked would not be appropriate for Alexa since she is without a living father. I am sincerely thankful that they thought of her situation. However, it is all around awkward! She was ultimately sent home with a bunch of items that said "Happy Grandfather's Day" for my dad. Again, this was greatly appreciated, whether it was an awkward situation or not.

The day came. Instead of sitting home, we celebrated with

another father in our lives. I'm still getting used this whole blended family/dating with children thing, or whatever you want to call it. The man in my life may not be my child's father, but he is a father and I am happy to have celebrated it with him. I enjoyed the day and never felt like Alexa and I were missing out. I will admit to feeling slightly guilty, but her dad is not here. We need to enjoy our time with the people who are.

We had a great day, and then stopped to visit Alex. I still don't know how much Alexa understands, but we brought him a gift, said hi, and wished him a happy Father's Day. He may not be around to raise her, but he is always going to be her father. Just when I thought I had gotten through the holiday, something else hit me. I dropped her off at daycare today to find another "daddy" drawing in her cubby. This time it said "Alexa and daddy." Daddy was then crossed out and changed to "mommy." I know it was a mistake they attempted to fix, but it hurt! Chalk it up to another odd experience.

I will close by saying happy Father's Day to my dad. He has been there with me for the best and worst moments of my life. He's an amazing man and I am so thankful he's mine. Alexa is so lucky to have him as her grandfather.

July 2014

Tuesday, July 1st, 2014 at 12:28 pm
The Summer of George

(Please note the Seinfeld reference)

This is the summer of Heather and Alexa. Okay so I do have a job and responsibilities and I'm not single, but still. Last summer, I just existed. I went through the motions and attempted to have some fun. We went to the beach and pool a few times, but just like the rest of the months last year, I wished them away. This year is different.

I swore that I learned to enjoy every moment and live life to the fullest. I said that I truly understood that life is short. I do and I will follow through. I'm taking every opportunity to enjoy this summer and I'm tanner than I have been in ten years! I'm having fun, enjoying life, and enjoying every day with my little girl. I'm loving watching every new experience.

I've never been to the beach so many times in a short period. Even growing up in New Jersey, it's more fun now. So many moms tell me how tough it is to take a child to the beach with so much stuff to bring and it isn't so relaxing. Well, I disagree. It is much more fun with a child! So what if my house isn't perfectly clean and the clean laundry is piling up again (even though there was none last week)? We are enjoying the sun and having great new experiences together.

I previously wrote about creating a bucket list. Last weekend I got to cross something off. I performed my first wedding ceremony. I was so excited to be a part of this and think it went great! This was the second wedding I attended since losing Alex. I did really well, mentally and emotionally. The only sadness I can speak of was watching the slideshow seeing the bride and groom with their daughter. The daddy/daughter photos started to get to me. I shed a few tears but still appreciated what it meant to them. It was a great day and I'm so honored to have been a part of it.

I know I've been slacking off with writing and all. I've just been busy with my normal life, plus enjoying the crap out of the summer!

Thursday, July 3rd, 2014 at 11:52 am
Mental Illness, or Not?

It should not be surprising that I am a member of many Facebook groups related to widowhood, young widowhood, suicide survivors, etc. A post caught my eye today as I was scrolling through my newsfeed. A woman was stating that she was leaving a suicide support group because she was tired of defending that her son was NOT mentally ill. She attributes his suicide to a medication he was taking and finds it insulting that people would say he was mentally ill. Clearly, I do not find it insulting to use the term mentally ill, as I use it regularly. Statistics state that 90% of suicides are as a result of mental illness. Am I certain that Alex was within the 90%? No, probably not.

A while back, I tried to convince myself that his suicide was caused by something else. I found many supplements and herbal products that belonged to him. I knew he was taking vitamins, but did not really know what. I found after extensive research that one of the ingredients had been linked to some suicides. Can I be certain that this was the cause? No, I cannot. Would it make a difference if this was the cause?

I had been told by people in his life that before we had met, Alex was suspected as Bipolar. I have previously written how now, in hindsight, it would make a lot of sense. He fit the description and symptoms to a T. If this were his diagnosis, it would certainly explain many other things in our life. Again, can I be certain that this is what was the cause? Nope, I still can't.

A few years before his death, Alex was convinced he had a head injury. He kept describing that something was wrong with him. Our family doctor stated he had depression, but Alex denied it and it was never mentioned again. Can I ascertain that the cause was depression? Beyond a reasonable doubt? No.

This illustrates my point exactly. Does it really matter? If

I knew the exact cause, would it change anything? No, he would still be gone.

Suicide survivors join groups to support each other. We have all been affected by a similar tragedy. We all understand the negative stigma associated with suicide and do not want to see our loved ones thought of in that manner. To me, the term mental illness is not negative. People do not choose to be mentally ill, as much as they do not choose to be ill in any other way. It is a disease, just like any other. It saddens me to hear someone find it offensive. It doesn't make you any less of an intelligent, wonderful person.

I'm starting to wonder if it is time for me to move on from these groups. It helped so much in the beginning, but now I feel it brings me down. So many people feel they are defined by their loss. Though it is a big part of who I am, it is not everything.

Saturday, July 12th, 2014 at 1:00 pm
Happy Birthday, Mow

Birthday week was rough. Alex would have turned thirty-one on the 6th. Fourth of July weekend was always about celebrating his birthday. My, how things have changed. I really don't have much to say except I did the best I could. Last year, I made a huge party and celebrated him. This year, I hid from it and tried to have a normal day, weekend, and week.

The day passed and I did okay. I shed a few tears but nothing major. The days after, I was in a funk. I can't describe it other than I was mad, missed him, and now feel guilty when I do.

Life has changed so much and I'm so lucky to have found happiness again, but it doesn't just make it go away. In some ways, it makes it more complicated. It feels weird to love someone here, yet miss someone on the other side at the same time. I've said it before and I'll say it again. It all comes down to the fact that it is two totally separate things. This week, I thought over and over again how my daughter said, "Happy birthday daddy" to a grave. This haunts me. We're getting closer each day to a time when she will understand. It freaks me out to say the least.

I got through a few crappy, cranky days and I'm doing better. I'm looking forward to a great weekend. Happy birthday to my angel on the other side. <3

August 2014

Monday, August 25th, 2014 at 8:35 pm
Time Flies When You're Having Fun?

Wow, it certainly is not like me not to have an update in a month. What has gone on in the past month? The biggest thing that I am sure many are interested in my opinion on is the death of Robin Williams. I have seen so much positivity, yet also so much negativity discussed around it.

I was certainly saddened to hear that the world lost another brilliant and intelligent man to suicide. Someone else lost their husband and someone else lost their father. I have traveled that path and do not wish that upon anyone. I hope he found the peace he was looking for and that in time to come, his family will be able to forgive him and make peace with it as well.

I always hoped that some good would come from Alex's death and I hope the same comes from this loss. A good man lost his life to a tragic illness. That is how we should see suicide, and maybe this is shedding some light on mental illness. He had it all. Family, fortune, fame and yet still succumbed to the unbearable pain of depression.

All the publicity of this took its toll on me for sure. It reminded me of the past tragedy I lived through. It opened up more and more thoughts about mental illness and suicide. It was all over Facebook, the radio, and the TV. I could not escape it, but in the end, I think we can all learn something from this. No one is exempt. Mental illness can affect anyone.

As usual, people had the typical opinion that suicide is selfish. I was thrilled to see some incredible articles disproving that theory.

Where is my life at? Well, in the same place it has been. I am happy and continuing to move forward each day. I admit willingly and without shame that I am still in therapy and still medicated, and it makes a world of difference. I am a happier person and a better mom admitting that I still need these things to be mentally healthy since Alex's death. I've said it before and I will say it again. I will never be the same, but I know that I am meant to go on and will be okay. I guess I should say that I AM okay. I've never really considered myself a sensitive or anxious person, but tragedy has changed me, for the good and the not-so-good alike.

I'm greatly enjoying summer! I have written in the past about how I have a hard time with winter. I have the opposite thoughts during summer. It's brighter out longer. It's warmer. I can go to the beach, the park, and just play in the backyard. I've spent a lot of time with friends and family just enjoying this season. I hate to see it leave, but am hopeful for a better winter this year. Last year was certainly better than the one before!

So yes, overall, time flies when you're having fun!

September 2014

Thursday, September 18ᵗʰ, 2014 at 7:53 pm
The Grass is Always Greener

I may have used that title before but it fits.

I don't think it would be entirely appropriate for me to hijack someone else's words for my blog, but I would like to summarize something I found on a "Young Widows and Widowers" page that I felt compelled to respond to.

The "rant," as it was self-named, began with frustration toward the term "single parent." I have also had an issue with this term. The classification of single parent leaves you open to so many assumptions. Though I'm not sure I would like to walk saying "widowed parent" either. Also, am I no longer a single parent because I am in a relationship? All of this nomenclature confuses me and I would like to stick with, "I'm a parent."

Here are the issues brought up by this fellow widow/parent:

1. She does not have the freedom other single parents have when their children are with the other parent. She would LOVE if she had that time.

2. Divorced parents act like they know what she goes through. She feels that they are not single parents, but as shared parents do not deserve said title.

3. She did not choose to be a single parent like the other kind of single parent had.

Many comments followed with people agreeing and venting about how unfair it is and how much worse we have it than others, etc.

Here are my two cents:

I agree. It is totally different and I did not sign up to do this alone, but I did choose to have a child for better or for worse. I wanted her no matter what life brought. Though I'm doing it alone, I'm thankful for every moment with her. It is difficult for all of us to deal with doing this on our own. We don't get a break when they go off to see their other parent like divorced parents do. We have to make all decisions on our own and take on the role of both parents. Sometimes it sucks, but think about this. The divorced parent has to spend a portion of their time without their child. They CANNOT see their own child sometimes. That doesn't happen to us. No one else has a say in what we do with our children or how we raise them. Many of them did not choose that life either. The grass is always greener.

In the past, someone commented on how lucky I was to not have to share my daughter. I was highly offended. However, as time has passed, I realize that comment should not have been so offensive. What I have been through is terrible. I don't wish it upon anyone. I would never choose to be widowed or wish death upon the parent of any child. However, if I can choose one major thing I am lucky for, it's my daughter. Yes, I'm lucky to not have to share her as many single parents do.

Thursday, September 25th, 2014 at 1:30 pm
Suicide Prevention Month

September is Suicide Prevention and Awareness month. It is a tough month for survivors, but also brings out the best. It is a time of remembrance. For me, it is a reminder to keep fighting for awareness and push to save lives. It helps me to tell my story in hopes it will help someone else. This month brought a lot of people out of their shells to tell me their stories and how I have inspired or helped them. This means more to me than I can ever put into words. I am your average survivor. I just chose to speak out and make my struggle public. It means the world that my story can make a difference in someone's life.

All over the country, there is one day when people light candles to honor and remember their loved ones. I was at work but still lit a candle, and asked my friends and family to do the same. My Facebook was hopping with tags of people lighting a candle for Alex. It was such a mix-up of happy and sad at the same time. We were all virtually together honoring someone we loved. I felt so supported and that together, we were making a difference.

October 2014

Thursday, October 16th, 2014 at 6:47 pm
Strange How Your Mind Works

I drive past the funeral home from Alex's funeral often. Most of the time I hardly notice and if I do, I don't really think much of it. Other days are different. I drive past and see myself laying on the ground in the parking lot that day. I see the fountain and am reminded of staring into it in such a complete haze. I remember the stairs so well, dragging myself up them the night of the private viewing. A lot of those days are a blur, being truly some of the worst days of my life. I struggle to remember the details, yet I struggle to forget them too.

Tuesday, October 28th, 2014 at 11:35 am
Brave?

Warning… This post has some rather strong opinions in it.

All over the news, Facebook and even on the cover of People magazine is a woman planning to complete suicide. She has a plan, a date, a method, etc.

In this instance, why are we glorifying suicide? They are putting this woman on a pedestal and writing about how brave she is for her choice, while looking down on, judging, and condemning others who have chosen this path. Because she has cancer? It's okay if you have an illness? How is that any different from choosing to die instead of suffering from and living with mental illness? Why is this woman being honored, yet others are chastised?

She has been diagnosed with terminal brain cancer. Though I know this is the exception to the rule, people do survive this! People do beat the odds! People live years and years of happy lives long after this diagnosis. How do I know? I've seen it happen with the exact same diagnosis. I can't imagine not wanting to fight!

As a veterinary technician, I am obviously in favor of euthanasia as the end of suffering. I do believe that physician-assisted suicide is a wonderful thing in the end. When there is no quality of life left and the end is near, we should have the right to go peacefully in our sleep instead of suffering until the last second. When it comes to cancer, the end is agony, and I think it's a wonderful thing we can do to end suffering. I'll say it again, in the end.

This woman has a long way to go until that point. However, that's MY opinion.

All in all, who are we to judge? People like Alex and Robin Williams were called cowards and selfish, while she's called brave. Who are we to decide who deserves praise versus who we vilify?

◆◆◆

December 2014

Thursday, December 18th, 2014 at 1:58 pm
December

Here we are. It's December again and people are wondering and asking how I am doing with it all. I know the dreaded date is coming and I'm worried how I will handle it this year. I'm not going on vacation, but still plan on hiding away from my house for a few days. I am working on New Year's Eve and worry about it feeling too similar to that day. That's what I did. I got up, went to work, came home, and then it all happened.

Last year, I made a special meal and honored him. This year, I'm tempted to say I'm over it. Not to say I'm over what happened, but how many times do I put myself through the agony of a memorial? This year, I want it to just be New Year's. I know that is not logical and it will never just be New Year's, but there is more happiness this year than the past two.

When it comes to Alex, I've been in the anger zone a lot lately and I don't really feel like thinking about all of this. Mean? Maybe, but there comes a point when it's old and annoying. I don't want my life to revolve around this. I've rebuilt my life and I'm happy. Yet, I will forever have this major bump in the road, major mark on my soul, and major dent in my sanity. I don't want it and I didn't deserve it, but it is what it is.

The time is coming closer and closer to having to do some explaining to Alexa. She is clearly confused about what a dad is, who her dad is, and what a family consists of. How much does a two-year-old understand and how much do I fight her on knowing the truth? The truth is, I'm not so sure anymore. Alex will always be her father, but he's not the one raising her. I am.

Recently, someone told me that they wished we could have Alex back for a day. This really got me thinking because at this point in my life, I don't want that. I have nothing left to say and feel like my wounds are slowly healing. Why would I want to open them again?

I've lived my life and raised my daughter without him for almost two years now. I think I've done a pretty good job. I'm starting to understand letting go of the past and moving forward.

January 2015

Thursday, January 1st, 2015 at 3:23 pm
Two Years and a New Year

Some days I really think you are a piece of shit for doing this to me, especially on a holiday. What a low blow dirty move! Ruin the life I had and every New Year's to come, even after I've rebuilt my life. Yesterday was one of those days.

Then, of course, I came to my senses and realized all the stuff I've been fighting for. You made a mistake in a dark moment. You were sick and in pain and couldn't see what you were doing to the people around you and blah, blah, blah.

I've been doing well, living life, and am not a mess

anymore. Somehow, I convinced myself that yesterday would be the same. I'll be fine! Well, yes and no.

I purposely spent the night away from home, as to not wake up in my house. I feared it would be too similar to that day. I got up, got ready for work, and got Alexa ready for daycare. I was fine until I backed out of the driveway. Then, I lost it. I cried and cried bringing Alexa into daycare and through the Dunkin drive-thru. I don't even really know why.

I decided I should stop, take a break, and calm myself with a smoke. I know not the healthiest choice, but my choice nonetheless. At that point, it became apparent that I didn't have a lighter. I had somewhat calmed myself down and realized I still had some time, so I ran into the grocery store, grabbed a lighter, and got in the only line open. The woman in front of me had a decent number of items. She then picked up another item and asked for the price. Upon hearing the price, she decided she didn't want it, but then the cashier realized the price was wrong. She picked up the item again (a window candle) and found that it was on clearance. The woman got excited and ran back for more. She was digging and counting and announced, "Well I have 41 windows in my house!"

O...M...G! I asked if there was another register open. Nope. I asked if I could go to customer service. Nope. I asked if I could just have a pack of matches. Nope.

They slowly began unpacking the boxes one by one, swiped, and then manually discounted them. I was so frustrated by this point that I burst into tears. Yup, really, I did.

Finally, they opened another register for me and after fourteen minutes, I left with my lighter. Thankfully, that was the worst part of my day. I got through the work day okay and had a pretty decent night overall. I was asleep by 11 pm.

Each year gets a little better. I'm so thankful for all who were there for me, checked in on me, and distracted me. Yet, I'm shocked at those who seemed to have forgotten. Happy New

Year. I'm looking forward to what 2015 has to bring.

Wednesday, January 21st, 2015 at 1:36 pm
How Did I Get Here?

How did I get here? Here I am again, almost thirty-one years old and single. It wasn't supposed to be that way. I got married somewhat young and that was supposed to be it. We had nothing and built a life together. I couldn't imagine loving again after him, yet I did. I thought I was so lucky to find someone who could deal with my past and wanted to start a new life with me. It turns out, love wasn't enough and I'm left shattered and alone again, with no control over the situation. I can't help but wonder what is wrong with me and what have I done to deserve to be unhappy.

I've been through much worse and I survived. I will be just fine. Though I lost another part of my heart and soul (two parts this time)and a year of my life wasted.

Thursday, January 22nd, 2015 at 2:02 pm
Advice?

It's interesting to me how over the last few days, so many people have come to me with their thoughts and praise. I've been repeatedly told how strong I am, as I have heard many times before. I AM a strong person and I can make it on my own. That doesn't mean I'm not hurting.

I was told that I always give the best advice in these situations and now I need to take that advice.

What advice do I have for myself right now? You can always see things more clearly when you're on the outside. Well, life is unfair. You live and you learn. Someday, the pain will be replaced with happy memories. Pick yourself up, brush yourself off, and have some fun. You only live once, so enjoy it! All in all, everything is okay in the end. If it's not okay, it's not the end.

I'm finding it very difficult to not blame Alex. If he weren't gone, I wouldn't be in this situation.

I am so lucky to have my little girl. I'm not sure how much she understands, but she knows I'm upset. She's the best thing I could ever ask for and even now tells me to "just keep swimming."

Saturday, January 31st, 2015 at 1:47 am
A Good Man

Alex did some really crappy stuff sometimes. He wasn't perfect and made mistakes. He tried his best and sometimes failed. He hurt me in a way that I will never fully recover from…

However, he loved me with all that he had. He wanted me and wanted to be with me. He created a life with me with no doubts. He was thrilled to marry me. He reminded me that he loved me and looked forward to the time we spent together. He appreciated who I am and what I've done for him. He tried to give me everything I ever wanted, even when sometimes he couldn't. I truly believe his suicide was an attempt to make MY life better. He told me that himself.

I always felt that he was looking down, cheering me on. I believed that he was going to work some magic from the other side and fix what he did. I accept that the choices I make (as well as others around me) are beyond his control, but I still ask that he lead me. Each day, I wonder the meaning and reason behind things that have happened. I wish he could answer that for me.

I have never been good with the unknown. I want to fast

forward life and see where it ends up. I want to know everything will be okay, but I can't. So for now, I have to relax and enjoy the ride.

February 2015

Thursday, February 26th, 2015 at 2:26 am
Nothing Can Touch Me

I'm feeling really good. That being said, I put almost half of the weight I lost back on in the past year. I've always struggled with my weight, but I am determined again.

I was feeling down, rejected, and just bad about myself and needed to do something about it. I'm already just a few pounds shy of back to my lowest weight and hope to push it further. I really despise exercise, but when it's all said and done, I feel great. I'm in a better mood and frame of mind. I have more energy, I'm less tired, and I'm proud of myself. I always like feeling like I look good too, but what girl doesn't?

I'm almost one-month smoke free. Many of you know how much of a sore subject that is. I started smoking again the day Alex died. Though I tried to quit a few times over the past couple years, I never really put my all into it and made it happen. This time, I'm doing it with no real incentive other than for myself. I've always known you can only quit when YOU want to and not for anyone else. I want to.

I have officially signed up to walk eighteen miles in an overnight walk for suicide prevention. When this journey started, I could not even finish a 5K. It may take some time and effort, but I know that I can and will do it! I will do it for Alex.

I have many failures in life. Don't we all? Every single one brings new knowledge. I'm still a strong, successful woman in so many ways.

I heard a song today that has always been inspirational to me. I don't really know why. I know that the true meaning of the song is different than my interpretation, but I will end with the lyrics.

"I am falling and if I let myself go, I'm the only one to blame! I'm safe up high. Nothing can touch me!"

April 2015

Friday, April 24th, 2015 at 1:21 am
Just...Like...Me...

I can make excuses over and over for all the reasons why I have not written anything lately. It has never been a secret that I mainly write when I am hurting, upset, and really need to get things off my chest. I've been doing very well lately. I am happy, all on my own, with Alexa of course.

I have been insanely busy with all my many endeavors, raising my daughter, and enjoying life. The nice weather is here and it always makes me feel better. I love being busy. I live for it. I take on more and more all the time. Though it becomes stressful at times, I wouldn't change it at all.

I wrote a lot in the beginning of this crazy journey. I was in a dark place and my blog was my therapy, my slight glimpse of hope and happiness for the future. My sanity hung on by a thread, and the blog strengthened that thread. I think it is a good thing that I don't need it as much anymore.

I have recently turned thirty-one. Scary right? It is. I really had a great birthday but will admit, depression followed for a few days. I don't know why a stupid number had me so down. I started to write about it, but realized I needed to suck it up and deal! I'm not going to get younger, no one does. Get over it. I can look at my life and say that I am not where I planned to be at my age, but so many of us aren't. Just because life is not what I pictured does not mean it is not a beautiful picture anyway. Besides all the leftover trauma and being alone, (blah blah blah) life is pretty awesome.

So, the real topic for tonight. My favorite show killed off one of my favorite characters, which made my other favorite character join the widow club. Of course, I cried, like many "Grey's Anatomy" lovers probably did as well. The one thing that really stood out to me was the realism. In every show, I find that when a woman finds out her husband has died (this seems to happen a lot on TV), they fall into hysteria instantly. There is instant screaming, crying, and over the top reactions. That makes sense when you imagine what it must be like.

As a woman who has experienced this, it's not like that. I was calm, shocked, matter of fact, and numb. Tears were impossible to produce, even if I tried. It struck me tonight when Meredith acted exactly the same way. I know she is not real, so someone did their homework when writing this episode. Seeing her this way hurt, and I felt that she was real. I felt myself thinking about what the next few hours, days, weeks of her life would be like. I felt like my friend joined my world. In one moment, she lost her husband and the father of her children, just like me.

I'm anxious to see what life has in store for her, so of course I'm looking forward to next Thursday's episode. It may be too much. It may hurt to watch her walk a similar path to mine. Though she is not real, I hurt for her. Though it may resurface old

Sunday, April 26th, 2015 at 10:32 pm
Really???

    Even two years later, things come up that never cease to amaze me. Alex was obviously the computer guy in the house. That was his job and that's what he knew. I know enough to get by, but never really had to learn major stuff. If anything went wrong with my computer, I would have him look at it. I do not know how to do a lot of administrator things and do not know passwords to many things. When it comes to our Mac, I know how to use Photoshop and that's about it. We each had our own login, but I hardly ever use mine. Photoshop is on his login and it has stayed that way. Thankfully, that is one password that I did know.

    Today, I needed Photoshop and I needed a photo from my email. I logged into his account and opened my email. Somehow, I never noticed the toolbars across the top where he had bookmarked pages. When it comes to curiosity killed the cat, I'm always the cat. I just can't help it.

    I clicked on My Sites. I shouldn't be surprised and nothing should anger me anymore at this point, but it did! Really? This is all he cared about.

    The list of bookmarks were as follows:

- Delaware Open Carry
- Delaware Concealed Carry Forum
- The Firearm Blog
- DefensiveCarry

- GunReview
- Gunsmithing
- First State Firearms
- Shooting: Both Eyes Open
- Fate Of Destinee *(Some chick obsessed with guns)*
- Handguns Magazine
- Learning to Appreciate Gun Rights the Hard Way
- Gun Current
- Secret Compartments - Hidden doors, secure stashes
- Dynamic Training Strategies
- Texasguntrainer.com/billofsale.pdf
- Firearms, Trading and Gear for the Average Joe
- Concealed Carry Resources
- Midway USA shooting supplies
- The Truth About Guns

I have no words.

August 2015

Tuesday, August 25th, 2015 at 1:30 pm
I'm Still Here!!

It's amazing how life works. I don't know any other way to describe it. Things have been great. Life was going so well. I was very much enjoying life on our own. I love being a mom and love my busy crazy life with all of my crazy endeavors. However, life has a way of throwing curve balls and I suddenly went from single mom, to building a new wonderful life with someone.

I am truly getting my second chance at a family and I can't put into words how this feels. Alex swept me off my feet and we instantly knew that this was it. You know what? It can happen twice. I used to scream at (what I imagined to be) Alex. I told him that after what he did to me, he owed me and needed to fix my life. This time, the months I spent single made me a happier, stronger person, completely comfortable with myself. I needed that, and now I believe that, when I was ready, Alex sent me the life I was eventually looking for, even if I didn't believe I quite wanted it yet. In the meantime, I've done so much!

I raised $2,200 for Suicide Prevention and walked eighteen miles overnight through Boston in Alex's memory, and in a freaking monsoon. No matter what, this is a huge part of me, and I will never stop.

Everything happens for a reason, the good, the bad, the indifferent. In the darkest moments of life, keep going! It WILL get better. Live every moment to the fullest! I know I am.

October 2015

Wednesday, October 7th, 2015 at 12:32 pm
Out With the Old

After almost five years in my house, it was time to move on. Even now, staring at the screen, there are so many thoughts and emotions to go with this change that I don't even know where to begin. First, it's exciting. I'm starting a new life with someone in a new home. Buying a house was truly a pain in the ass, but worth it. The house is beautiful and amazing and we so excited to be a "new family."

However, here are some thoughts about the old house. This was the last place Alex lived and the place he died. This is Alexa's first home and first room. There are so many happy and awful memories here. It's bittersweet to leave it all behind, even if only moving up the street.

For my long-term readers, you know what happened. You remember the shocking days after, trying to put all the pieces together and finding out just how many guns he had. I never knew about them, yet found them hidden all over my house. I thought for years this was long behind me, but it happened again.

One of the final things to move out of the house was his desk. Guess what? There was a gun hidden under the drawer! How did I never know that? I had a rush of anger and embarrassment in front of those helping me move. How many times had I used that desk? All I can say is WTF? Really??? This shit is still happening?! I just can't! I really thought that there was nothing I could be angry about anymore at this point, but clearly, I can.

Again, my long-term readers know my story and know that I don't hide from it. The good, the bad, the ugly, the indifferent, I put it all out there. Almost three years has passed and, until today, Alex's mess remained. Part of me is ashamed that I didn't take care of it previously, but it is what it is.

In the beginning, I couldn't bring myself to do it. A rug covered it and there it stayed, basically forgotten about. It's gone now, and I sit here not really knowing how I feel about it. When it comes to suicide, loved ones are left to figuratively and literally clean up your mess. Think about that. Really let that sink in. I would like to think that cleaning up his literal mess is the end of cleaning up any other messes related to this dent in my life.

For so long, I kept saying that my life was not what I wanted and not what I chose I chose the life I have now. I can finally say that, and it's exactly what I want.

December 2015

Wednesday, December 9th, 2015 at 4:16 pm
A Long December

Let me start out by saying that life is good and I am happy. I've been working so hard lately and so proud of my achievements. I have a beautiful new home, an amazing man and family by my side, and some of the best friends a girl could ask for. I'm so extraordinarily thankful for everything I have.

With that being said, December is hard. Being so happy in my new life, does not erase the pain, the trauma, and the memories of my old life. It's a dent that can never truly be fixed. Each day that comes closer to "that day" seems to get just a little bit harder. The anxiety is harder to ignore and I "just keep swimming" toward it.

I don't want to rush through the holidays, but then again, I really want to rush through the holidays. I am torn between loving the Christmas decorations and feeling as though they mock me when I drive by, reminding me of that night. Everything is just a tiny bit harder this month. All in all, I WILL make Christmas a good experience this year, even if just for the kids in my life. It's not about me, it's about them.

I posted something on Facebook recently regarding my feelings on guns. It was in regards to a child being shot by a "paranoid" man, legally carrying a gun. I know that no one can truly understand the thoughts in my head, but I thought this summed it up well. Nothing is black and white. There are so many grey areas. I lost someone I love because someone mentally unstable legally owned guns. Now this family did too. Let me be clear, I do not blame the gun and do not believe everyone needs to be disarmed. However, guns are not toys and often fall into the wrong hands. They have serious repercussions and maybe we need to stop the gun argument and try to see both sides.

To elaborate, I fully understand that owning and carrying a gun is 100% a personal choice and legal right. I do not think we should lose that right. I understand that the experiences people have in their lives mold their opinion on things. My personal opinion is as follows: The sole purpose of a gun is to inflict harm. You can argue that it is for protection, but it protects you by inflicting harm. I spent months hearing the "guns are safe" speech from Alex. In the end, that gun (and his unknown mental instability) took him away from me. Therefore, I do not welcome them in my home. It takes a split second for something to go wrong and I was never willing to take that risk, especially with children in the house.

I have PTSD. I am not crazy or irrational. I can take whatever comes at me and deal with it how I must. I do not expect people to change their views for me. However, I do expect mutual respect.

I took Alexa to Alex's grave yesterday to decorate for Christmas. I know that so many see this as completely heartbreaking and awful, but it is different for us.

This is normal. This is my life. This is all that she knows. She has no memory of him, therefore cannot be hurt by it. I feel that it is appropriate to teach her of his existence, and the respect that we show at his grave. I teach her the basics, and what I feel a three-year-old can understand. She asks some questions and then goes back to her day.

It is almost one year since I have smoked a cigarette. Some of these December days really make me want to give up, but I'm strong enough. I may eat some extra chocolate, but I'll be okay.

Everything comes down to the fact that I'll get through anything. I always do.

That was the last post I ever wrote. I'm not sure I ever made the conscious decision to stop writing. That's just how it happened. At the time I'm writing this, it has been two years (and two days) since the last post. It's not to say that I didn't have anything left to say or wanted to stop writing. I certainly didn't want to disappoint readers. I started to feel that I was at a different point in my life. I no longer saw each day as just surviving until the next. I no longer identified as just a widow. I was so much more. Life had changed and I moved forward. I started to feel that I could not be so raw, complete, and honest without it affecting other people in my life. Life wasn't just about me anymore, but the relationships I started and the people in my life. I didn't want it to affect them.

I also didn't want to be fake. I was always complete in my writing, never leaving anything out. I felt I could never be true to my posts while leaving things out. Not only that, the start of my blog was for me to heal, to get my thoughts out, and to have a place to express myself. This is not to say I still don't have these thoughts or that I have completely moved on. I don't think you ever completely move on. It's different now. It's not solely who I am. I had healed to a point where I did not NEED a constant avenue to express my thoughts and feelings. When something would arise that I needed to get out, I tended to just write a Facebook post.

Though the other goal of the blog hasn't gone away. I always wanted to make something positive of this experience, of the tragedy in my life. I always wanted to take the trauma that I lived, grow from it, and help others. I wanted to help people in a similar situation as mine and I wanted to show people what it was to be a product of suicide. I wanted to end the silence.

Things do come up that significantly affect me still. It's been five years and still, I have the reminder of my daughter every day. I have things that affect my relationship every day. I have fears that are directly related to what happened. Yes, I have worked through so much and I have changed my life extensively. I *have* survived and will continue to survive. It has gotten easier, or maybe the pain dulls. Still, it will always be a part of me, even if I have chosen not to identify as "just a widow."

I have completed another overnight walk through Washington DC, walking eighteen miles again and raising money for suicide prevention. That will always be with me. Those experiences will always have meaning, whether they are directly for Alex or not. It doesn't always have to be directly about *his* memory and losing *him*, though that is the driving force that started it all.

Suicide is HUGE. It affects so many people, whether it is someone who has lost a loved one, someone who has attempted, or someone who has struggled with depression and is unsure where to turn. It affects so many, yet still to this day, I feel it is something we hide from. We don't bring it up in conversation, unless it's a joke. We pretend it doesn't exist. We think it won't happen to us, and that it will never affect someone we know. It can, it will, and it does. I'll say it again, it affects SO MANY, so why are we silent about it? Why are we ashamed of it? Why do we hide from it? Though I don't walk into a room and say, "Hi, I'm a suicide widow," if it comes up, it comes up. I won't hide from it still to this day. I will talk about my experiences. While it may make someone uncomfortable, it may make someone else realize something. It may make someone else feel slightly better about their situation and less alone in their situation, knowing that I've been there too.

While my life isn't perfect, I have not fixed everything, and even though I do not believe in "happily ever after," I still like to say, I'm pretty darn close. I have moved on to a happy relationship, but that does not negate my marriage. I have started new paths in life, but that woman was still me. I do believe I am a different person than I was five years ago. How many of us are the same person after five years? Life is constantly changing and we are growing with it. We all have different experiences that led us to where we are now. We all make different choices in life. I am not the person I was five years ago, but I still identify with her. I'm still the woman that lived it, got through it, and survived. I'm happy to say that, at this point, I'm doing more than just surviving. I'm thriving.

My number one goal in life has to be happy with myself, happy with who I am, and happy with the person I had become. No one is perfect and I am certainly far from it. However, the goal still was to be happy with the person I am. I can honestly say I accept the mistakes I made along the way, but I know I had good intentions. I know I am doing right by his memory, right by his daughter, and doing my best to inspire others to do the same.

This blog was the true reality of the first three years of my journey in widowhood. Yes, I am a widow and I guess I'll always be a widow, whether I remarry or not. But I do not live my life as only that. I do not live my life with the main focus of widowhood. I move forward each day and see what life has to bring. The past two years have been the same. I've had some MAJOR ups and MAJOR downs and worked through them. I've worked every day to improve myself. That's not to say I was ever a bad person but I strive each day to be just a little bit better. We always have room for improvement and I'd like to be the best version of myself that I can be. I like to grow and change.

I like to try new adventures. I like to have new goals and dreams. One thing I have learned, and maybe it should not have taken tragedy to teach me, is you only live once! You have one chance to do what you want with this life. What is it that you want to do? What is it that you want to experience? What is it that you want to achieve? At twenty-eight years old, I felt that my life was exactly where I wanted it to be. I was married and had a child. I had a career and a house. Was that it? Was that all I was supposed to do with my life? For the moment, I was content with that. It was not until one night when everything changed and I had to start all over that I realized I have so much more to offer the world and so much more to offer myself. I have so much to experience in just one lifetime.

The first two years were a lot of figuring out how to survive and how to be a mom. Then again, I think all of us just figure it out as we go along. There is no manual that comes with having a child or losing a spouse. You do the best you can with what you were given. I was doing the best I could.

What did I want out of my life? I never really knew. I dabbled in all different things, figuring everything happens for a reason. Everything leads you somewhere, even if not to the original goal. Everything is going to fall into place some day. I wrote my blog. I continued my job. I succeeded in sales. For those who know me personally, you probably know me as the "candle girl," since I spent most of the past four years selling candles. Why? It was fun. It got me out of my comfort zone. I met new people. I found a hobby. I wasn't *just* a widow, mom, and Vet Tech. I had something else important to me, complete with goals to achieve. I'll forever be thankful for that experience.

With that, I kept expanding. Whether it was directly choosing to bring something else into my life or almost feeling like the world just put it in the right place, I've experienced so much. I'll never stop reaching for what's next. I'll never stop looking to experience something new. It's unfortunate to have had a tragedy show me I wanted more out of life, but I'm thankful for the realization. Who knows? Maybe I would have figured it out eventually anyway.

I am happy with who I am. I accept my faults and failures, and respect what they have taught me. I'm not happy for losing someone close to me, but I am grateful for the time we shared. To this point, life has not been what I expected. The life I had came crashing down, so I built a new one.

ACKNOWLEDGMENTS

My grandparents, Michael and Veronica Campanella, for their contribution to this project and major impact in our lives. Alexa and I are so lucky to have them.

Lisa Condora, for her encouragement throughout the journey and her deep involvement with this project through editing, her Foreword, and so much more. She was always one of the first to jump on the blog as soon as I posted. She was there for me during my worst moments, and my best moments. Contact her at www.condoracontent.com.

Liz Iorlano, for holding my hand through some of the hardest parts of my life and always reminding me to keep writing that blog! Also, her husband, Adam. Without him, I never would have met Alex! I will never be able to explain how thankful I am for that. They were also gracious enough to sponsor this book, to help me with the financial obligation that came along with it. They are amazing people with a special place in my heart. Adam is one of the few people I know with a goal-oriented drive, like mine. Help support his goals and dreams at www.buyacarfromadam.com.

My parents, Ray and Joan Lobby, for their love and support throughout life, motherhood, tragedy, and this journey. They have encouraged me to write the blog and pushed for the publication of this book. Both have been there through every step of the way. I don't know what I would do without them. Also, major love and thanks for my mother's company, Positive Energy and Vibes Reiki, for sponsoring this project.

My daughter, Alexa Cruz, for every day giving me a reason to go on, wiping my tears when I cried, even though she wasn't old enough to understand, and for at only five-years-old, telling me how proud she is of her mom.

Ken Hackett, for showing me that true love can happen twice and always loving me in some way over the past two and a half years. Thank you for being so encouraging and accepting of the choice to write this book. Thank you for being here for my dark moments, not just my bright ones. Thank you for being my chapter two. I love you.

Jessica Ryan, for being the only person to come to mind when asked who I wanted called that night. Thank you for literally holding me up when I didn't think I could stand on my own. So many moments were bearable just knowing you were there with me, whether physically or virtually.

The "Marlboro Crew." There are just too many of you to mention! Though we all met at different stages of childhood, we truly grew up and experienced the beginning of our adult lives together. When life took a terrible turn, you never left me behind, even having to travel so far to support me in person. I will always be grateful for the times we shared and will continue to share, no matter where life takes us.

Kiera Smale, for changing my perspective, changing my future, believing in me, and giving me the push I needed to get this book finished.

Kyleigh Twiford with Damsel in Defense. Though we met

selling candles, I am happy to support her new journey, as she does mine. Check out the great products for self-protection. This is something so very important for women and even more, single women. http://www.mydamselpro.net/PRO20662/.

Julie Edwards with Perfectly Posh. Julie came into my life at a later part of this journey. She has been such a wonderful, supportive friend from the moment we met. She's not "just another Posh girl." She's someone special. http://PerfectlyJulie.po.sh.

Love and thanks to contributors: Kristen Regan & Karen D'Alessandro

In Memory Of:

Chad A. Youngs - April 25, 1978 - February 28, 2016

John Edward Yearwood Sr. - October 8, 1964 - July 20, 1992

Benjamin David Butler - August 8, 1984 - July 19, 2002

Gordon Donald Armstrong, Jr. - September 1, 1997

Whitney Maher. "Whit, there's no difference in my eyes. We are still together in a different way. I love you." -Melissa

Bryan Gavin Moore - June 8, 1974 - September 2, 2017

"In loving memory of my mom, Rosemary Burton. She was amazing mother and grandmother. I can only hope to live my life with the grace and humor she lived in hers. 10-17-48 to 01-19-17." – Julie Edwards

Wayne "TT" Lewis - July 23, 1994 - August 29, 2015

Tabetha Mowrer - January 22, 1966 - January 5, 2012

In Memory of Joe Madeo - 2/2/85 - 3/20/14 "Thanks for giving me my inspiration." - Alicia McDaniels

Let's Keep This Conversation Going

Follow my blog at: thewidownextdoor.com

Contact me on my Facebook page
Facebook.com/thewidownextdoor

Ignite your light with me at: HeatherCruzIYLC.com

You are not alone. You cannot be replaced. Confidential help is available for free.

National Suicide Prevention Lifeline
1-800-273-8255
suicidepreventionlifeline.org/

None of us will ever forget your ability to light up a room with your smile, how you could learn anything you wanted to, and master it in no time, and your dedication to everyone you loved. You gave me the best gift I could ever ask for, our little girl. She's amazing and I know you're shining your light on her. You'll always be in the hearts of everyone you touched. The world lost an amazing person way too soon.